A PHOTO

MAMMALS
OF
NEW ZEALAND

CAROLYN M. KING
PHOTOGRAPHS BY ROD MORRIS

NEW
HOLLAND

First published in 2008 by New Holland Publishers (NZ) Ltd
Auckland • Sydney • London • Cape Town

www.newhollandpublishers.co.nz

218 Lake Road, Northcote, Auckland 0627, New Zealand
Unit 1, 66 Gibbes Street, Chatswood, NSW 2067, Australia
86–88 Edgware Road, London W2 2EA, United Kingdom
80 McKenzie Street, Cape Town 8001, South Africa

Publishing manager: Matt Turner
Editing and design: Punaromia

National Library of New Zealand Cataloguing-in-Publication Data

King, C. M. (Carolyn M.)
A photographic guide to mammals of New Zealand / Carolyn M. King.
Includes bibliographical references and index.
978-1-86966- 202-8
1. Mammals—New Zealand. 2. Mammals—New Zealand—
Pictorial works. 1. Title.
599.00993—dc 22

10 9 8 7 6 5 4 3 2 1

Colour reproduction by Pica Digital Pte Ltd, Singapore
Printed by Times Offset (M) Sdn Bhd, Malaysia, on paper sourced from
sustainable forests.

Front cover photograph: dusky dolphins (*Lagenorhynchus obscurus*), Kaikoura
      (Dennis Buurman Photography www.dennisbuurman.co.nz)
Back cover photograph: rabbit (*Oryctolagus cuniculus*)
Spine photograph: weasel (*Mustela nivalis*)
Title page photograph: Weddell seal (*Leptonychotes weddellii*)

Contents

Introduction

What is a mammal?

Literally, mammals are animals with mammary glands; that is, the females feed their young on milk. Mammary glands have evolved from sweat glands, and the earliest kind of milk simply oozed out on to the mother's belly skin. The young just licked it up, much as a modern dog will lick the salt off a sweaty hand. (Nipples merely channel the milk, and they were added later.) In almost all other respects, the modern mammals and their ancestors are immensely diverse. We now recognise three distinct living groups, but there were once many more that we know only as fossils.

Mammals evolved from an ancient group of **therapsids**, descended from the very earliest egg-laying vertebrates alongside but independently of the reptiles. Therapsids appeared about 250 million years ago, as cousins to the true reptiles evolving along an entirely separate lineage; but they laid eggs in a nest, as do reptiles and birds. Their descendants, the very first and most **archaic mammals**, are all now entirely extinct. They were small, mouse-sized creatures that lived for 100 million years in the shadow of the dinosaurs. These little creatures were completely unlike any kind of mammal living today. Very little is known about them except that they could have lived almost anywhere in the world, including the land that later became known as New Zealand.

Almost all modern mammals retain their fertilised eggs internally and incubate them in a uterus, rather than externally in a nest. There must have been a period of transition from one state to the other. We can deduce something about how it happened by observing the most primitive group of living mammals, the **monotremes**. They originated in Australia more than 200 million years ago, and were once abundant and diverse, but they are represented now only by the echidnas and the duck-billed platypus. Monotremes are certainly mammals, because they secrete milk from simple mammary glands

Elephant seal pup with penguins.

without nipples, but they still lay eggs, like the therapsids did. Their descendants still survive in Australia, the only place where these remarkable, invaluable glimpses into evolutionary history may still be seen in the flesh.

The second and third living groups are represented by the two main kinds of living mammals: the **placentals**, which bear their young in a uterus, and the **marsupials**, which bear them in a pouch. Both originated in the northern hemisphere: marsupials in what is now North America, and placental mammals in Asia. Their last common ancestor lived about 190 million years ago, and they have evolved separately ever since. Early marsupials or their ancestors spread to Gondwana (the combined continents of the southern hemisphere) before it became cut off from the northern continents about 170 million years ago, but most placentals remained confined to the north for many millions of years more. The cosmic impact of 65 million years ago that finished off the dinosaurs also swept away the last of the ancient marsupials of North America.

In the southern hemisphere, the marsupials became very widespread and diverse. They spread across South America, and reached Antarctica/Australia (still joined together) along what later became the Antarctic Peninsula (40-million-year-old fossil marsupials have been found there). South America, cut off from the northern hemisphere about 130 million years ago, became an island continent when the link with Antarctica was broken about 35 million years ago. In splendid isolation for the next 30 million years, South American marsupials and a few placentals became wonderfully diverse and successful. Then, about 5 million years ago, the new Panama land-bridge opened the way for a mass invasion of new and more advanced placental mammals from the north (the American opossum was one of few southern marsupials to make the return journey).

Monotremes, marsupials, and primitive mammals continued to thrive in Australia, and also in Antarctica until it froze about 14 million years ago. After that, the primitive mammals disappeared, leaving no modern descendants at all. Only in Australia did marsupials and monotremes remain secure, and they survived until placentals eventually reached the island continent in human times.

Mammals in New Zealand

Modern New Zealand is a large fragment of land and continental shelf which began to split off from the rest of Gondwana about 80 million years ago, while Australia and Antarctica were still joined. The parts that were above sea level were thickly forested, and inhabited by representatives of the ancient Gondwanan fauna and flora. The gap that opened up as New Zealand drifted away, now called the Tasman Sea, was over 1000 km wide by 65 million years ago.

The first people to settle in New Zealand arrived a mere 800 years ago, and the only living mammals they found were placentals that could swim or fly across the Tasman Sea (bats, seals and sea lions, whales and dolphins). There were no marsupials, and no four-footed land mammals of any kind. For decades, biogeographers

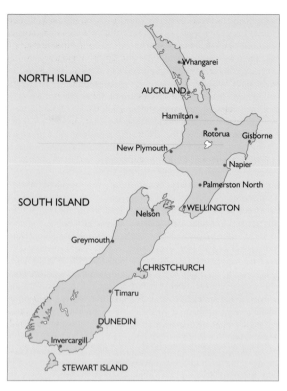

NORTH ISLAND

- Whangarei
- AUCKLAND
- Hamilton
- Rotorua
- Gisborne
- New Plymouth
- Napier
- Palmerston North

SOUTH ISLAND

- Nelson
- WELLINGTON
- Greymouth
- CHRISTCHURCH
- Timaru
- DUNEDIN
- Invercargill
- STEWART ISLAND

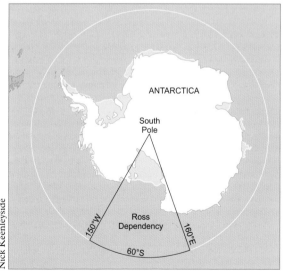

ANTARCTICA

South Pole

150°W

Ross Dependency

160°E

60°S

have assumed that the reason that land mammals (and snakes) were absent from New Zealand is that their ancestors all 'missed the boat'. But in fact the earliest mammals (monotremes, marsupials and their archaic ancestors) were already well established in Australia long before 80 million years ago, so perhaps there was another explanation: maybe there *were* land mammals in New Zealand before it was isolated, but they have no living descendants and we had not yet found any fossils showing that they were ever here.

In 2006, this possibility was confirmed; a paper was published describing three fragments of a hitherto unknown archaic mammal (not an ordinary mouse, or a marsupial; indeed, it is apparently unrelated to any known group) that were found in fossil deposits in the South Island, about 16 million years old. The implication is that tiny non-flying land animals belonging to an archaic, mystery species were indeed living in New Zealand at the time it separated from the rest of the world, and they came along for the ride. Even more intriguing, it suggests that their lineage survived for some 60-odd million years, including throughout a period around 25 million years ago when most of the land surface was under water.

After such a marathon survival story, it is tragic that these fascinating little animals did not survive long enough for us to meet them, but merely left their fossils to intrigue us. Maybe it was the ice ages that finished them off; whatever the reason, they died out, and New Zealand became, alone among all substantial land masses on earth, dominated by birds. Mammals were represented only by thousands of bats pouring out of caves and tree roosts, while seasonal assemblages of breeding fur seals and sea lions gathered on rocky shores and beaches, and dolphins and whales romped offshore in their thousands. When the Polynesians arrived in the late AD 1200s, they brought rats and dogs, the very first four-footed placental land mammals to establish permanent populations in New Zealand; some 600 years later, successive waves of Europeans brought many more, from all around the world.

The species brought in with human help (by definition **'introduced'**) fall into three main groups. Some were released by accident: rats, mice and cats lived and bred on ships, and could not have been prevented from disembarking in numbers, even if anyone had thought of trying to stop them. A second and much larger group included species carefully chosen from among the cream of the world's most 'useful' animals, by settlers with good intentions but absolutely no way to predict what might happen when possums, rabbits, goats and deer were released in this wonderful new country. These species and others were deliberately transported, often at great expense, and no one was more amazed than their previous supporters to see how completely differently they behaved from the way they did (and do) at home. The third group were the passage-paid experts brought in to control those of their predecessors that had done too much going forth and multiplying. The stoat, weasel and ferret were expected to manage the numbers of rabbits; too late it became clear that, in fact, rabbits determine the numbers of their predators, not vice versa.

Why the mammals of New Zealand are unique

The net result of New Zealand's peculiar history and geography is that the combination of mammalian species in the New Zealand Region (the **'fauna'**) is unique in the world, for several reasons.

First, the New Zealand Region (see maps p. 6) includes not only the North and South Islands (the **'mainland'**, total 269,000 sq km), but also (1) 735 inshore and offshore **islands** of up to 1 ha in area, ranging in latitude from the subtropical Kermadec group (Raoul and Macauley) through the Chathams (800 km east of Christchurch) and Stewart Island (30 km south of the South Island) to the subantarctic groups (Snares, Auckland, Campbell, Antipodes and Bounty Islands) and (2) the **Ross Dependency**, a triangular chunk of the southern hemisphere from latitude 60°S to the South Pole between longitudes 160°E and 150°W (total 414, 000 sq km). It includes the Ross Ice Shelf and two important Antarctic research stations. Three other islands, Macquarie, Lord Howe and Norfolk Island, are part of the same geographic region but administered from Australia, so are not included here.

All this wonderfully diverse geography means that the habitats offered to mammals in the New Zealand region range from temperate coastal bush to high mountains covered in permanent snow, from tropical forests to thick sea ice, from improved farmland to huge pine plantations, from limestone caves with constant temperature to semi-arid tussocklands with severe winters and hot summers, from swamps to massive freshwater lakes, from small island refuges to modern cities. Mammals of one sort or another live in all of these places except the lakes, so the variety of animals described here is impressive. On the other hand, mammals that have reached previously untouched offshore islands have done terrible damage in the past, and increasing numbers of islands are being cleared of mammals in order to prepare them as refuges for beleaguered native species that cannot survive on the mainland. All human

Norway rat, a significant predator of native fauna including weta.

visitors to islands (especially those sailing in or fishing from private vessels) should be extremely careful to avoid accidentally helping any unwelcome hitchhikers get ashore.

Second, virtually all the mammal faunas of other nations include some introduced species, but New Zealand is the only country in which the non-native species are completely dominant (in numbers both of species and of individuals) over the native species. **'Native'** in this context means any species whose ancestors evolved here or arrived without human help, and which now maintains independent populations in the wild. In modern New Zealand, that means only bats, seals and sea lions (including those confined to Antarctica), dolphins and whales. Regrettably, all these are scarce or hard to find; almost anywhere you look, the only mammals you are likely to see will all be introduced.

Third, because New Zealand's marine mammals are all by definition good travellers, few belong to that special subgroup classed as **'endemic'**; that is, found nowhere else in the world. A species can be endemic to various extents; if its members are only slightly different from their nearest relatives elsewhere, they may be endemic only at the subspecies or species level. The more different they are (which usually means the longer they have lived isolated from their relatives), the higher up the taxonomic scale their species is placed, through genus to family level or above. Of the native mammals, the New Zealand long-tailed bat, the New Zealand fur seal, and the Hector's and Maui's dolphins are endemic at species level; Hooker's sea lion is endemic at genus level; and (the longest-resident and most special of all) the two short-tailed bats are endemic at family level; but the whales and other dolphins mentioned here live not only in New Zealand waters but elsewhere as well.

Fourth, most introduced species were chosen to serve human purposes. Polynesians brought their companion animals, but they had few options. Europeans had vastly greater choice, but their decisions were inevitably captive to the assumptions of their age. As they saw it, their task was to create a 'Britain of the South' without the crippling social restrictions of the original. When they arrived and found that nature had carelessly omitted to stock New Zealand with game for hunting and predators to control pests, the settlers assumed they had to supply them.

Consequently, most introduced species brought in by Europeans were relatively large animals. The smallest of those they deliberately introduced were rabbits and hedgehogs, followed later by weasels and stoats; certainly, none of the teeming hordes of northern hemisphere voles, lemmings or wood mice were ever considered. By contrast, terrestrial mammalian faunas assembled by natural processes are dominated by small species. In Britain, almost two-thirds of the 63 resident land-breeding species are small (up to 1 kg body weight), compared with less than a quarter of New Zealand's 45 resident land-breeding species. Had rats and mice not so often stowed away on ships and canoes, and scrambled ashore in droves at every opportunity, New Zealand might still be the only country in the world with no small rodents.

This great shortage of small mammals in New Zealand forests had unexpected and tragic consequences when stoats arrived in 1884; the staple prey of stoats in the northern hemisphere were voles, and in their absence, stoats found feral house mice (smaller, less meaty and much less abundant) to be an unreliable and inadequate substitute. For at least the last 120 years, the occasional **irruptions** of mice in beech forests after a heavy seedfall have served to produce matching irruptions in the numbers of stoats, without distracting their attention from eating birds.

Fifth, the long voyage under sail endured by the founding groups of many introduced mammals had one interesting consequence that no one anticipated. Regular cleaning of cages and stalls was necessary to enable the human passengers to cope with the animal smells, and the soiled bedding was thrown overboard – complete with the eggs and larvae of many parasites. Various serious animal diseases were also eliminated from among the live cargo, simply by the higher mortality of infected individuals. The effect was the same as that of a remarkably strict quarantine, and it meant that the surviving animals were an exceptionally healthy lot. The unexpected benefit is that their descendants in New Zealand are free of the problems that still plague their ancestors; for example, the hedgehog and the rabbit lost their specific fleas, and chamois are free of sarcoptic mange. Even possums, which had a much shorter journey, carry only a third as many species of parasites in New Zealand as their relatives do in Australia.

In modern times this quarantine effect has had further unexpected consequences for management of pest mammals, both bad and good. Attempts to introduce myxomatosis into New Zealand in the 1950s failed, because a blood-sucking vector, the specific European rabbit flea, is required to transmit the myxoma virus (in Australia there are enough mosquitoes to do the job instead). Contemporary research on biological control of possums is investigating how parasites imported from Australia might be used to carry anti-fertility agents.

Sixth, New Zealand was the last substantial land mass in the world to be settled by people. It is the largest by far of the Pacific islands to be colonised by the Polynesians, but also the coldest. Organised settlement by Europeans began in New Zealand a full 60 years after the first convict ships landed their reluctant passengers in Australia. This late start did at least mean that successive New Zealand governments could avoid some of the mistakes made by other colonial powers, including the importation of mammalian species that have caused havoc elsewhere. The list of prohibited species has been extended over the years, and now includes the European red fox and mole, the Indian mongoose, the South American coypu, and the North American mink, grey squirrel and muskrat. Serious though the problems caused by our existing pests are – especially possums, rabbits, rats, goats and red deer – we have cause to be grateful that the New Zealand fauna does not include any of these other internationally famous pest species.

How to use this book

Purpose and descriptions

This book illustrates and describes most of the native and introduced mammals that inhabit or visit the mainland of New Zealand, its offshore and outlying islands, the Ross Dependency in Antarctica, and all their surrounding seas. Each entry presents information in the same order, unless it is inappropriate or simply unavailable.

Species are listed in conventional taxonomic order, without unnecessary detail such as taxonomic authorities, and with little concern for current debates about phylogenetic relationships. Each group of related species is introduced with a brief list of features they have in common. Species which are always under direct human control (livestock, farm dogs, pets and the like) or are unlikely to be seen without special equipment (those which are very rare, extinct or live in inaccessible places) are excluded.

Like people, most species have two formal names, equivalent to a personal name and a surname, but for animals the names are in Latin. By convention, the surname (the **genus**) is given first with a capital, followed by the species name, always without a capital. As in a human family, species belonging to the same genus are more closely related than species in different genera.

Some species include **subspecies**, which have their own extra name. Because they are or once were geographically separate, they are distinctly different from each other, in appearance or in genetic make-up or both, but they cannot for various reasons be promoted to full species. Most subspecific distinctions are ignored here, unless there are reasons to mention them. For example, the two subspecies of Hector's dolphin are similar in appearance but genetically distinct; both are endangered, but the North Island subspecies (Maui's dolphin) is *critically* endangered; likewise, two of the three subspecies of the New Zealand lesser short-tailed bat are at greater risk of extinction than the third one. Contrariwise, two apparently distinct species of deer (red deer and wapiti) were introduced separately from Scotland and Canada, but they turned out to be fully interfertile subspecies of a single circumpolar species *Cervus elaphus*.

The standard subheadings are as follows:

Identification A concise description of physical features, including **dental formula** and behaviour where that might help identification.

Similar species Many of the mammals included are universally familiar, but others come in groups of similar species (rats, mustelids, bovids, deer, dolphins and whales), so for them a succinct list of the differences between them is given.

Size Measurements are given only broadly, in units appropriate to the size of the animals, and without specifying variation unless there is a large difference between males and females. If some measurements are not given, it means there are no suitable data.

NZ range Includes place(s) of origin and history of arrival or release, if known.

Habitat The main environments where you might expect to find the species within its New Zealand range.

Food Diet and feeding behaviour.

Reproduction and **Populations** Breeding and population data, like measurements, should be taken as approximate only. This is sometimes because detailed information does not exist, so what is given may be very rough; more usually, it is because the body size, breeding rate and population dynamics of most mammal species are all strongly affected by food supplies, which vary with season, year and social status. Estimates of numbers or density are given only where available. For further details, consult the reference sources quoted in the list of Further Reading.

Status Each species is assigned to one of five categories defined in the Glossary (native, endemic, vagrant, introduced, feral).

Management Each species is assigned to one of four categories defined in the Glossary (Protected, Pest, Major pest, Mixed pest and resource). A major pest is defined somewhat loosely as a species causing damage of national rather than local significance and requiring management at substantial cost. Species regarded as a resource only (such as farm stock) are not included here, but for species which have both resource value and pest status, the somewhat surprising category 'Mixed' is necessary. In New Zealand, far more than in other countries, many species of mammals are valued by some people and abhorred by others, according to where they are found. So, for example, hunters and conservationists disagree about limiting the spread of game species (especially deer, tahr and pigs) into new areas. Only in certain established areas, and for special negotiated purposes, are long-term compromises possible. For example, conservationists give hunters priority in the Blue Mountains (a designated Recreational Hunting Area), and hunters give conservationists priority in Takahe Valley (the last stronghold of a specially protected native bird).

The book is not a full field guide, nor has room for illustrations of skulls, footprints, scats/faecal pellets/nests/food remains etc., but some of these details are given in the source publications.

The **Glossary** explains technical terms used in some of the descriptions.

Reporting observations

Mammal watching in New Zealand is nowhere near as well supported as bird watching, which means that almost anything could be worth reporting. Readers of this book are strongly encouraged to contact either of the authors or the publisher's office to describe whatever they have seen that could be potentially interesting. In particular, any carcase of a native species, any bat roost, and most urgently any actual or potential **strandings** of cetaceans should be reported immediately to the nearest Department of Conservation (DoC) office, or call the DoC emergency number, 0800 36 24 68.

Important warnings

Many species of mammals in New Zealand are regarded as serious pests, for reasons explained in these pages. Organised control operations against pest mammals are done on a very large scale in New Zealand, using a variety of powerful **traps and poisons**. People using the back country should be careful to obey public notices warning of control operations, avoid touching any trap or bait station, and be especially vigilant in preventing children or dogs from doing so. Even non-toxic baits or 'chew cards', used to estimate numbers of pests remaining after a control operation, should be left strictly alone. Carcases of possums or ferrets, especially those with visible swellings, could be infected with bovine TB and should not be touched.

On the other hand, many species of mammals in New Zealand – often the same ones – are also regarded as valuable resources, especially by recreational hunters. Access to wild game is much easier than in the northern hemisphere, but it is not entirely free. For information about hunting permits, ask at any DoC office.

Brushtail possum eating mistletoe.

Marsupials: wallabies and possums

Order Marsupialia

All female mammals support their young through two main phases of growth: gestation (pregnancy) and lactation (suckling). Placental mammals are so called because the placenta provides a sort of docking mechanism, linking the mother's bloodstream with that of the foetus. The mother can provide nutrients and oxygen, and remove wastes, for months at a time. The young are safer inside than outside, and can develop further, so gestation in placentals can be longer than lactation. By contrast, marsupials have only a simple yolk-like placenta that cannot connect with the mother's bloodstream, so, for them, gestation must be short. Instead, they have evolved a long and very complex system of lactation. The marsupial strategy is not inherently more 'primitive'; their lineage is the same length as that of placentals, and in their different way, marsupials have been an immensely successful and diverse group.

Young marsupials are tiny at birth (sometimes less than 1 g). The newborn climbs unaided into an external pouch and locks onto a nipple supplying energy-rich, low-fat milk; meanwhile, its older sibling, which has recently left the pouch, can still reach in to the other nipple for supplies of high-fat milk.

The most familiar marsupials are the kangaroos and wallabies (the difference depends mainly on size). There are around 60 living species, and many more are known as fossils. Their most obvious character is their large hind feet (the family name means 'big foot'), which are used to thump the ground as an alarm signal. Nine species were introduced into New Zealand in the 19th century, but only two made it to the main islands; the rest either failed to establish or have remained confined to offshore islands. Of five other marsupial species brought in, only the brushtail possum survived.

Parma wallaby *Macropus parma*

Family Macropodidae. **Identification** Grey-brown above, pale grey below except for white throat; a distinct white cheek stripe; tail tip often white, relatively hairless; short, rounded ears; often sit back on their haunches with tail between legs. Dental formula I1/3, C0/0, Pm1/1, M4/4 = 14. **Similar species** Dama wallaby has reddish patches on shoulders; Bennett's wallaby much larger, South Island only; brush-tailed rock wallaby has a bushy tail, does not sit propped on it; swamp wallaby has a yellow cheek stripe. **Size** Males about 4.5 kg, 49 cm long, tail 48 cm; females 3.5 kg, 45 cm long, tail 44 cm. **NZ range** Kawau Island only. First released about 1870, along with 3–4 other wallaby species. **Habitat** In tall kanuka/tairaire forest, or in dense undergrowth in exotic forest. **Food** Grass, herbs and weeds. **Social behaviour** Solitary, nocturnal, rather timid. Easily displaced by the more aggressive dama wallaby. Resting sites under thick cover, never shared. **Reproduction** Females reach breeding age at 2–3 years (later than in Australia), males at 1 year. Breeding season long but variable; young can appear

at almost any time. Gestation 42 days, pouch life about 210 days. **Populations** Average life expectancy of a 6 month old estimated at 2.7 years; maximum >9 years. **Status** Introduced. **Management** Pest (except 1969–84). If the technical difference between parma and dama was known when parma were brought to Kawau Island, it was forgotten for decades. Only the islanders noticed two types of small wallabies, the 'small brown' and the 'silver grey', both included in routine control operations on Kawau 1923–69. In 1965 the parma was 'rediscovered' on Kawau, by zoologists examining skins and skulls collected during culling. This announcement caused a sensation, because by then the parma was believed extinct in Australia. At IUCN's request, Kawau's parma were protected in 1969; 736 Kawau parma were exported alive to captive breeding programmes around the world and to re-establish the species in its original habitat. But in 1972, adequate surviving populations of parma were found in Australia, removing need to release stock from Kawau there. Parma removed from IUCN's list of threatened species; protection of Kawau's parma ceased in 1984. Unlike dama and brush-tailed rock wallabies, parma are not included in the repatriation programme preceding the planned eradication of all wallabies from Kawau Island.

15

Dama wallaby *Macropus eugenii*

Female.

Family Macropodidae. **Identification** Grey-brown above, pale grey below, reddish patches on shoulders; tapering tail grey-brown, furred to end, often used as a prop; long pointed ears. Dental formula I1/3, C0/0, Pm1/1, M4/4 = 14. Molar tooth row moves forward through life, providing continually renewed chewing surface and a method of estimating age. **Similar species** Bennett's wallaby much larger, South Island only; parma wallaby has a white cheek stripe, white chest; brush-tailed rock wallaby has a bushy tail, does not sit propped on it; swamp wallaby has a yellow cheek stripe. **Size** Males average 3.5–5.5 kg, 90–100 cm long, tail *c.* 40 cm; females 3–4.5 kg, 85–90 cm long, tail 35 cm. **NZ range** Kawau Island and locally in North Island. First released on Kawau Island about 1870, then at Lake Okareka (near Rotorua) in 1912. At least three other wallaby species also released on Kawau, but dama still the only one on mainland North Island. Present distribution: on Kawau, mainly on the drier upland areas; on the mainland, about 1700 sq km around the Rotorua lakes, still expanding (sightings possible outside this area). Current control operations expected to reduce this area in future. **Habitat** Prefers places with dense cover for daytime resting, within reach of pastures for grazing at night. Exotic forest acceptable, especially when plantations young or where roadside weeds/grass available. **Food** Primarily grasses, fallen leaves, tree seedlings. Capable of conserving water from fresh vegetation, so can survive without drinking for long periods. **Social behaviour** Sociable, nocturnal. Regular resting sites used by groups of both sexes, all ages. Individuals recognise each other by nose-touching. Social hierarchy maintained by submissive displays (lowering the head), fights rare. **Reproduction** Females mature at 1 year; gestation 28 days; births mainly January–March; single young remains in pouch on average 250 days. Most females mate again within 24 hours, but implantation delayed for up to 11 months. In December/January, the long days of summer reactivate the blastocyst and the next young appears a month later. Almost all mature females breed every year, and most live only 1–2 years. **Status** Introduced. **Management** Pest. Probably less damaging than pest ungulates, but dama limit regeneration in native forest, and would prevent recovery of protected areas unless removed. Both on the mainland and on Kawau, control of wallabies is a high priority for local authorities, although difficult to achieve because (1) Kawau is large enough (2257 ha) to support thousands of wallabies, and (2) dama are valued in Australia (the population supplying the ancestors of the New Zealand dama is extinct). In 2003, the Pohutukawa Trust repatriated 60 dama from Kawau to Australia. Eradication of the remainder is scheduled.

Juvenile.

Bennett's wallaby *Macropus rufogriseus*

Family Macropodidae. **Identification** Large wallaby with long fur, mostly grey-brown but slightly reddish on shoulders and pale grey below, black feet; tail tapering, furred to end and darker at tip, sometimes used to support body when sitting. Dental formula I1/3, C0/0, Pm1/1, M4/4 = 14. **Similar species** No other wallaby found in South Island. **Size** Males average 12–21 kg, 140 cm long including tail; females 10–14 kg, 125 cm long. **NZ range** South Canterbury. First liberated on eastern Hunter's Hills in 1874. Founder stock <3–5 pairs, probably from Tasmania. Now occupy about 400,000 ha bounded to north and south by Rangitata and Waitaki Rivers, and to east and west by the coast and Lake Tekapo. Still spreading along Sherwood and Two Thumb Ranges. **Habitat** Occupies mountain ranges to 2000 m, covered with tall tussock grass, with flax, scrub or remnant forest in gullies. Survives heavy frosts in shaded rest areas during winter. **Food** Grazes on grass, hawkweed, clover; browses

matagouri, *Celmisia*, many broadleaf forest species. On sheep pasture, feeds at night on many of the same species that sheep take by day. **Social behaviour** Solitary, except during breeding season (February–March), nocturnal. Neighbours identified by scent signals, generally avoided. When necessary, stand-up fights (often over access to females) involve biting, kicking, fur-pulling, ending when one signals submission by turning head away, and is then chased off. Several males follow every oestrus female, and dispute access to her.

Female.

Reproduction Both sexes fully mature at 2 years; gestation 26 days; births mainly February–March. A single young remains in pouch on average 274 days, attached to the teat for the first 50–75 days, eyes closed until 135–150 days, naked until 165–175 days, emerging in November–December. Development of the next young, following a post-partum mating, delayed by lactation until the next season. **Populations** Birth rate high, and mortality independent of age. **Status** Introduced. **Management** Pest. Since 1940s, accused of fouling sheep feed, damaging fences, destroying crops. Remarkable numbers of Bennett's removed during control programmes since then. Over 10 years 1947–56 some 100,000 were shot by ground hunters; over 15–20 years after 1971, 2500–3000 a year (about 20% of the population); in 2002, 862 in 11.5 hours from a helicopter. All these operations had minimal effect, largely because wallabies are good at demographic compensation: the higher the losses, the higher the replacement rate. Eradication not feasible at present.

Joey in pouch.

Brush-tailed rock wallaby *Petrogale penicillata*

Blue Gum Pictures

Family Macropodidae. **Identification** Bluish-grey above, reddish on rump and upper tail; face dark with paler cheeks; tail bushy, black tip, used for steering and balance when hopping but not to support body when sitting. Dental formula I1/3, C0/0, Pm1/1, M4/4 = 14. **Similar species** All other wallabies in NZ have tapering, non-bushy tails. **Size** Males average 5–7 kg, 55 cm long, tail *c.* 50 cm; females 4–6 kg, 50 cm, 45 cm. **NZ range** Kawau Island, and formerly also Motutapu and Rangitoto Islands (connected by natural causeway built when Rangitoto appeared out of sea during volcanic eruption *c.* AD 1400). Released on Kawau about 1870, and on Motutapu 1873. Rapidly colonised Rangitoto across causeway, abundant there by 1912; eradicated from both islands 1990s, but not at that time from Kawau. **Habitat** Prefers well-vegetated cliff faces or steep hillsides; some survive in pine forests on Kawau. Climbs sloping trunks of trees to rest in branches; juveniles occasionally become trapped there. **Food** Selectively browses several important native trees, including pohutukawa and rata, but also needs grass for adequate diet. On Motutapu, sunny cliff faces dotted with pohutukawa and backed by extensive pasture were ideal. Continuous forest on Rangitoto was probably not sufficient alone, since wallabies living there used to trek across the causeway to Motutapu to graze. Still, browsing by wallabies (and possums) was serious enough to interfere with forest structure on Rangitoto. **Social behaviour** Sociable, nocturnal. Individuals recognise each other by touching noses. Groups have well-defined social hierarchy, strongly enforced around resting/den areas (especially safe, sunny sheltered spots among rocks or under tree roots on cliffs). Social interactions range from mutual grooming through hissing to fur-

20

pulling, boxing and an occasional all-out fight, unless averted by submissive behaviour (turning head away). **Reproduction** When well fed, females mature at 1 year, young born any time of year. Age at first breeding, length of season and proportion of females producing young all decline when food supplies poor (i.e. where grass scarce, as on Rangitoto before eradication). Females receptive for only a few hours at a time, so males check them constantly. **Populations** In optimum habitat on Motutapu in 1970s, when brush-tailed rock wallabies were abundant (*c.* 12/ha), few lived more than 4 years. Numbers on Kawau never that high, perhaps limited by shortage of dens or competition with other wallaby species. **Status** Introduced. **Management** Pest. On Motutapu, rock wallabies hastened erosion of cliffs by undermining tree roots for den sites. Along with possums, they also competed with stock for grass, and damaged pohutukawa flowering. On Rangitoto both species prevented internationally important studies of natural sequence of revegetation of bare scoria after the eruption of AD 1400. Eradication by DoC on the two islands began with aerial drop of 28 tonnes of 1080 baits in November 1990. The survivors (*c.* 7%) were mopped up with intensive ground operations (traps and dogs), completed in 1999. Similar damage observed to lesser extent on Kawau. Current control programme on Kawau began with live capture and repatriation of rock wallabies to Australia (see dama wallaby); eradication of the remainder is scheduled.

Swamp wallaby *Wallabia bicolor*

Family Macropodidae. **Identification** Dark grey back, orange on belly and around ears, yellow cheek stripe; tail furred to end, dark grey to black. Dental formula I1/3, C0/0, Pm1/1, M4/4 = 14. **Similar species** Dama wallaby has reddish patches on shoulders; Bennett's wallaby white on belly, South Island only; parma wallaby has a white cheek stripe and white throat; brush-tailed rock wallaby has a bushy tail, does not sit propped on it. **Size** Males *c.* 13 kg, 80 cm long, tail 70 cm; females 10 kg, 70 cm long, tail 50 cm. **NZ range** Kawau Island only, mostly at the northern end. First released about 1870, at same time as 3–4 other wallaby species. **Habitat** Prefers thick scrub; avoids open pasture. Kawau probably never a good habitat for swamp wallabies; most forest already cleared for farming by the time they arrived, and remaining forest had none of the thick, diverse understorey they need. They survive in nearest equivalent, kanuka scrub on northern side. **Food** Primarily a browser, taking leaves from shrubs such as mingimingi and low trees such as karaka, but little grass; bark from pine seedlings; bracken and fungi. **Social behaviour** Solitary except when breeding; largely but not only nocturnal. **Status** Introduced. **Management** Pest. Does little additional damage compared with that done by other wallabies on Kawau, but planned restoration of island ecosystem requires them to be removed along with the rest. Not endangered in Australia, so not included in pre-eradication repatriation programme.

Swamp wallaby.

Brushtail possum *Trichosurus vulpecula*

Family Phalangeridae. **Identification** Large upright ears, large brown eyes; pointed face with strong whiskers; close woolly fur; grasping hands with strong non-retractable claws, feet, tail tip all naked underneath. Body colour varies from grey through deep brown to almost black; underneath, grey-white or yellow, blacks ruddy brown; tail black in all, occasionally with white tip. Belly, pouch area often stained. Dental formula I3/2, C1/0, Pm2/1, M4/4 = 34. **Similar species** Cat-like at a distance, but cats move more gracefully on ground. Cat tail furred to the end; claws retractable. **Size** Typical average 2.5–3 kg, range 1.5–6.5 kg; 65–90 cm long including tail 25–40 cm, generally larger in South Island. **NZ range** Introduced from Australia/Tasmania 1858 onwards to establish a fur trade; progeny spread around NZ with human help, especially

1890–1940. Now present in all suitable habitats on mainland NZ and on about seven offshore islands. Absent above tree line and from parts of South Westland, Fiordland. **Habitat** Forest, scrub of all kinds; every type of open grassland from tussock to improved pasture; arable crops; exotic plantations, orchards, shelter belts, swamps, sand dunes, suburban gardens. Best combination food/shelter, highest numbers, at bush/pasture margin. Tolerates heavy rain, frost and snow. **Food** Browses leaves, fruit, buds, flowers, bark, ferns, fungi, of whatever species is locally avail-

Four-month-old joey out of pouch.

Black form.

23

able; in places where preferred species (rata, five-finger, fuchsia, mistletoe) still survive, will remove every fruit and new shoot until the entire crop is gone and plants die. Also take meat, including birds and eggs, carrion (including deer/pig carcasses infected with TB), snails, stick insects, cicadas, weta and beetles. **Social behaviour** Solitary except during breeding season (February–March). Nocturnal, relatively sedentary but may make excursions of 1–2 km in a night. Residents communicate by scent and vocal signals giving information on age, sex, social status; avoid each other most of the time. Dens in hollow trees or among thick epiphytes; under thick ground cover or in burrows made by rabbits or kiwi; in haystacks, log piles or ceilings. Individuals use 5–10 different dens, none exclusively, defended only when in residence. Unless dens scarce, shared only with own young or prospective mate. **Reproduction** Onset of breeding season triggered by shortening days of late summer. No pair bond; high-ranking males get first access to females. Both sexes mature at 1–2 years. Oestrus cycle lasts 26 days, pregnancy 34 days; most females produce one young

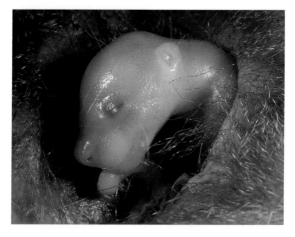

every autumn (April–June) from age 2 to 10. When food supplies good, some females will breed again in spring. Young born at 0.2 g, after 17–18 days gestation; climbs to pouch, locks onto teat for next *c.* 70 days. Fur visible at 90–100 days, eyes open 100–110 days; leaves pouch to ride mother's back after *c.* 120–140 days; weaned after 170–240 days. Dispersing young (mostly males) establish new homes *c.* 5 km away; most females stay near their mothers. **Populations** Numbers variable, but average 10–12/ha in podocarp/broadleaf forest; 1–3/ha in pine plantations, 0.5/ha in beech forest, 1–5/ha on farmland (up to 25/ha on bush-pasture margin). Almost half any given population will be under 2 years old (mostly males); some live to 14 years (mostly females). Average natural mortality rate 15–30%/year in adults; lower in pouch young, higher in newly emerged young and older adults. **Status** Introduced. **Management** Protected until 1947, now a major pest. Selective browsing by possums (and deer) has changed forest composition and killed trees over much of mainland; accelerated erosion on hillsides; damaged native fauna by removing their food, killing eggs and chicks; ruined crops and plantation forests; and cost tens of millions of dollars a year for control operations and lost production values. Eradication is, at present, possible only in three circumstances: on offshore islands (about 16 islands cleared so far, including four of very high conservation value: Rangitoto-Motutapu, Kapiti, and Codfish); in intensively managed conservation areas; and inside fences. TB first found in possums 1967; since 1999, intensive possum control (with beneficial consequences for native forests and wildlife) has rapidly reduced TB infection in livestock. If the internationally accepted level of TB in livestock defining TB-free status (0.2%) is achieved as expected by 2012, and possum control then slackens off, the consequences for native forests and wildlife could be serious.

Grey form.

Hedgehogs

Order Insectivora: insect eaters

Insects may provide abundant food in summer, but are inconveniently scarce in bad weather or in winter. Some animals dependent on insects can drastically (>90%) reduce their energy requirements by going into torpor until things improve. Daily torpor is a short-term response; seasonal torpor (hibernation) takes more preparation but enables insectivores to survive winter in cold climates. Hedgehogs may hibernate for months, but even they awake and forage periodically.

Hedgehog *Erinaceus europaeus*

Male.

Family Erinaceidae. **Identification** Grey-brown back covered with sharp, hollow spines *c.* 2–2.5 cm long; pointed face, small black eyes, short rounded ears; coarsely hairy face and underside; feet hairless, black; short black tail. When disturbed, uses a powerful dorsal muscle to roll itself into an impenetrable prickly ball. Agile despite clumsy appearance; swims and climbs well; easily travels 1 km or more per night. Dental formula I3/2, C1/1, Pm3/2, M3/3 = 36. **Similar species** None. **Size** Weight (both sexes) averages 650 g, range 300–1300 g; length 22 cm, tail 2 cm. Weight varies with season, as they lay up fat for winter and lose it while hibernating. **NZ range** Introduced by British settlers from 1870 onwards, at first for nostalgic reasons, later and repeatedly to control garden pests. Now found throughout lowland districts of both main islands plus Chatham, Stewart, D'Urville, Waiheke, Rabbit (Nelson) and Motutapu Islands. Absent from Fiordland, higher parts of Southern Alps and central North Island plateau. **Habitat** Primary needs are for plenty of soft food and dry nest sites. Ideal habitat is warm, moist lowland dairy pasture with few frosts and many snails, or gardens with food and nest sites supplemented by humans. Cannot survive in areas with more than 250 frosty days or more than 2500 mm of rain a year; elsewhere, numbers decline with altitude. **Food** Primarily small invertebrates, especially beetles, molluscs, worms, grasshoppers, caterpillars, weta; also mice, lizards, frogs, eggs, chicks, and carrion; in gardens, they prefer cat food to bread and milk, but devour either. **Social behaviour** Solitary, largely nocturnal. Dens usually constructed against a supporting wall or log, or in a rabbit burrow; range from light summer day-beds through stronger breeding nests to substantial winter nests or hibernacula. Dens not shared except by females with young. Hibernation hazardous, especially for small young (under 300 g), so avoided if earth temperatures remain above 10–11°C. Where hibernation is necessary, can survive 100 days in torpor if sufficient extra fat stored. **Reproduction** Breeding season long, mating promiscuous; gestation 31–35 days; litter size 4–7 usually reduced to 2–3 by high nestling mortality. Young blind, 15–21 g at birth, spines emerge within 36 hours; roll up after 11 days, eyes open at 14 days. Leave nest at 3–4 weeks, independent at 6–7 weeks. **Populations** Local resident populations mostly 1–5/ha depending on habitat, not counting numerous non-residents. Average lifespan in NZ 2–2.5 years. Compared with UK, NZ hedgehogs carry more mange mites but fewer fleas, and are much more often killed on roads. **Status** Introduced. **Management** Pest. Predation on ground-nesting bird nests can be common (20–80% of all predation losses). Control operations remove resident hedgehogs first, then collect many non-residents as they pass through, so sometimes report huge catches, especially in mild climates, e.g. 761 from Trounson Kauri Park over 3 years, or 400 from near dotterel nests in Northland. Tolerant of many toxins, so management, if required, best achieved by fencing or intensive trapping.

Nine-day-old young.

27

Bats

Order Chiroptera

Of about 1000 species of bats in the world, Australia has at least 90, but New Zealand has only three, all derived from wind-blown Australian strays, and they are now endemic to New Zealand. Other species probably also made the trip, but only these three have settled in New Zealand for long enough to become distinct from their ancestors. All are classed as threatened species, and one (*Mystacina robusta*, the greater New Zealand short-tailed bat) is probably already extinct.

Bats have the same problems of unreliable food supply as do other insect-eaters, but flying is a much more expensive way of getting about. They can easily slip in and out of short-term (daily) torpor, and some hibernate for several days at a time, but they cannot afford to sleep for too long.

Family Vespertilionidae

The sole member of this family in New Zealand is the New Zealand long-tailed bat.

New Zealand long-tailed bat *Chalinolobus tuberculatus*

Family Vespertilionidae. **Identification** Females a rich chestnut colour, males darker, underparts pale in both; limbs, wings, tail membrane naked, black. Long tail entirely enclosed in tail membrane. High forehead, small eyes, short broad ears; fleshy lobe on lower ear margin, also at corner of mouth. Small clawed thumb projects from wrist (halfway along wing). Dental formula I2/3, C1/1, Pm2/2, M3/3 = 34. **Similar species** NZ short-tailed bat has last 7 mm of tail free of caudal membrane. **Size** Weight 9–12 g; head–body length 42–63 mm; wingspan 240–300 mm. **NZ range** Evolved in NZ from an Australian species of this genus that arrived unaided sometime during the last million years. Still widely distributed in mainland and Stewart Island forests, but much scarcer than even 20 years ago. **Habitat** Native forest of all sorts, sea level to tree line; some exotic forests, e.g. along straight-line canopy breaks cut by roads. Prefers to roost in small, dry, well-insulated cavities well above ground level, such as knotholes, caves, or rock crevices in cliff

Male.

28

faces. **Food** Insects caught on the wing by echolocation, especially craneflies, moths, beetles. Temperature, wind strength, cloud cover, moonlight and activity of invertebrates influence when and for how long bats fly each night. In cold weather, saves energy by slipping into torpor by day. Foraging ranges of neighbouring social groups overlap. **Social behaviour** Sociable, nocturnal. Social groups complex, can number in hundreds. Members of smaller subgroups roost together or alone, often changing group composition and moving almost daily between roosting sites. **Reproduction** Females over 2–3 years old produce single young every November–December. Female can carry her non-flying young till they exceed 80% of her body weight; young can fly at *c.* 5 weeks old. **Populations** Common throughout NZ in 1800s, but now rare or gone from 13 of 15 sites surveyed in South Island since 1990. Fortunately, long-tailed bats are long-lived for such small animals. In Eglinton Valley, more than half of 107 adult females banded in 1994 still alive after 6 years; oldest known wild bat was aged 11 years in 2004. Survival highest in best habitat (and consequently, in bats in best condition, with safest, warmest roost sites); lowest in irruption years when stoats and/or rats abundant. Possums and rats in forest,

and pigeons, sparrows and wasps on cliff faces, exclude bats from otherwise suitable roost sites. **Status** Endemic. **Management** Protected. Classed by DoC as Nationally Vulnerable in North Island, and Nationally Endangered in South Island.

Family Mystacinidae

The ancestral form arrived in New Zealand from Australia at least 35 million years ago; its descendants evolved into two species of New Zealand short-tailed bats, one with three recognisable subspecies. The Australian lineage (known from fossils) is now extinct. Evolution in such prolonged isolation has made New Zealand short-tails different from any other bats in the world (they are endemic at family level).

New Zealand lesser short-tailed bat *Mystacina tuberculata*

Family Mystacinidae. **Identification** Grey-brown, stocky body; ears, wings, nose, legs, tail all bare. Large oval ears, prominent warty nostrils, small dark eyes. Short tail partly enclosed within tail membrane, partly (7 mm) free. When not in flight, wings fold under protection of thicker leading edge. Forearm, wrist with projecting clawed thumb (forming a front 'foot'), hind legs and well-clawed hind feet, all remarkably strong; these bats scuttle along on all fours almost as rapidly as mice. Dental formula I1/1, C1/1, Pm2/2, M3/3 = 28. **Similar species** NZ long-tailed bat has a long tail, entirely enclosed in caudal membrane. **Size** Weight 12–16 g; head–body length 60–70 mm; wingspan 280–300 mm. Three recognised subspecies, differing in geographic range and also slightly in size. **NZ range** Truly endemic (evolved in NZ). Formerly throughout all forests of mainland and Stewart Island, and presumably also inshore islands; now confined to nine locations in the North Island, two in the South Island, and two islands (Little Barrier and Codfish). Three subspecies recognised: *M. t. rhyacobia* in North Island south of Auckland, *M. t. aupourica* on Little Barrier Island and in Northland; and *M. t. tuberculata* in South Island and Codfish Island. Within the subspecies, there are at least six separate genetic lineages. These, and the curious distributions of the subspecies, reflect the long history of short-tail bats in NZ. Their ancestors lived through a very long sequence of drastic landscape changes caused by glaciation and catastrophic volcanic eruptions, inducing a complex series of local extinctions, migrations and recolonisations. **Habitat** Needs large (>1000 ha) blocks of native forest including many old-growth trees with epiphytes and cavities for colonial roosts. May move from high altitude to lowest available forest in winter. **Food** Forages both by echolocation during flight, and on ground by ear and scent; brushy tongue extrudes 5 mm beyond muzzle through gap between front teeth. Takes both insects (beetles, moths, flies, cockroaches and weta) and nectar, pollen and fruit (the only temperate echolocating

M. t. rhyacobia *adult and young.*

bat known to do so). Visits large flowers with exposed pollen, accessible nectar such as rata, pohutukawa; native wood rose depends on bats for pollination. **Social behaviour** Sociable, nocturnal. Roosts alone or in groups, in cavities in old trees or caves. Day roosts often solitary, but best colonial roost

M. t. auporica *feeding on wood rose.*

sites used by large groups (potentially thousands) for 5–10 days at a time, then all move on together. In winter, become torpid on many days, or hibernate for several days at a time, depending on the weather, but less often when huddling in a group. **Reproduction** Courting males 'sing' near colonial roosts to attract passing females. Most females mate in late summer, but gestation delayed until spring; single pup born December–January. All pups of group gathered in maternity roost for 2–4 weeks (carried there hanging by milk teeth from mother's teat). Mothers roost with them, or at least frequently visit roost to feed own pup. Pups 5 g at birth, blind; eyes open, fur grows *c.* 2 weeks; fully furred, flying by 4 weeks; full size but still lighter than adults by 8 weeks. **Populations** Central North Island once supported at least 12.5 million lesser short-tails; now <40,000 remain

M. t. tuberculata *showing robust limbs.*

(NZ total *c.* 50,000). Surviving 13 known populations occupy 100–150 sq km each, centred on colonial roost trees. Main cause of decline is deforestation; introduced predators may help to finish off small remnant populations. Lifespan, mortality rate unknown, since arm-bands used to mark other bats injure the wings of this species. **Status** Endemic. **Management** Protected. *M. t. rhyacobia* classed as Range Restricted, *M. t. aupourica* and *M. t. tuberculata* as Nationally Endangered.

Rabbits and hares

Order Lagomorpha

Like rodents, rabbits and hares have a huge pair of gnawing incisors at the front of the mouth with a large gap behind, and the canines have been lost. Unlike rodents, lagomorphs also have a second smaller pair of incisors. Both rabbits and hares process food twice to extract maximum value; after the first passage, soft green proto-faeces are immediately reingested; the familiar dark, hard faecal pellets are produced after the second passage.

In earlier times, fresh meat was highly valued by sailors, so domestic rabbits were spread around uninhabited islands to sustain survivors of shipwrecks. Rabbits and hares were brought to New Zealand in the 19th century to provide meat and sport for settlers.

Rabbit *Oryctolagus cuniculus*

Family Leporidae. **Identification** Grey-brown body, buff at nape of neck, white below; brown eyes; short tail brown above, fluffy white underneath; long ears with narrow black rim but no distinct black tip. Complex skin glands produce socially important scents. Eyeshine pink. Dental formula I2/1, C0/0, Pm3/2, M3/3 = 28. **Similar species** Brown hare larger, with longer, black-tipped ears, tail black above, and yellow eyes. **Size** Adults 1–2 kg, ears 60–70 mm, hind foot 75–95 mm. **NZ range** First introduced by James Cook in 1777, and by many others in pre-colonial times. Wild stock replaced domestic rabbits on mainland after 1850s, reaching all suitable habitat by 1950. Eradicated from 18 islands and died out on 10, but survive on another 25. **Habitat** Ideal habitat has short grassland

on light soil; scattered cover; a Mediterranean climate (as in parts of eastern mainland). They avoid cold, wet conditions, high alpine zone, damp, long-sward pasture, and closed-canopy forest. **Food** Introduced grass and herbs, including weeds. Can concentrate urine to survive on dry food alone if it contains at least 55% water. On improved pasture, 13 rabbits eat as much as one 50 kg sheep. **Social behaviour** Sociable, largely nocturnal. Live in groups of variable size, usually with a dominant pair and a social hierarchy among others. Communal warren (burrows), marked with scent signals. **Reproduction** Breeding season September–January in Otago, much longer in kinder conditions of North Island. Gestation 30 days; female produces 4–6 young in a separate short burrow, lined with grass and fur pulled from her belly; visits them for suckling once a night, blocks entrance with soil when leaving. Young blind, almost naked, 30–35 g at birth; eyes open 7 days, leave nest at 250 g, age 21 days; mature at 3–4 months, adult size at 6 months. **Populations** Rabbits reached legendary numbers in 1870s–1950s (e.g. 49/ha on one 2800 ha farm in 1912–13). Now, in most of North Island, resident populations of cats, ferrets and stoats can keep rabbits at tolerable levels all year round, maintained by steady supplies of young rabbits (in good conditions, rabbits breed 10 months a year and productivity can reach 42–48 young/female). In South Island the supply of young rabbits is lower (*c.* 23/female) and briefer (5 months). Predators have to hunt elsewhere during the 'off' season, so are not awaiting the next crop of young when they appear. Hence rabbits can reach high numbers in Otago, Canterbury and Marlborough. **Status** Introduced. **Management** Major pest. Damage to pastures led directly to demands for the introduction of mustelids. Massive, post-war aerial poisoning was largely successful in controlling numbers, but state-funded operations ceased in 1985. Rabbit haemorrhagic disease (RHD) was introduced illegally in 1997, and has effectively reduced both rabbit numbers and the amount of 1080 poison formerly used in rabbit control operations.

Young in nest.

Brown hare *Lepus europaeus*

Family Leporidae. **Identification** Tawny brown body, white below; yellow eyes; short tail white below, black above; long ears with distinct black patch at tip. Four toes in front, five behind. Dental formula I2/1, C0/0, Pm3/2, M3/3 = 28. **Similar species** Rabbit smaller, no clear black tip on ears, no black on tail, brown eyes. **Size** Adults 2.5–5 kg; ears 90–105 mm; hind foot 130–155 mm. **NZ range** Introduced repeatedly from mid-1860s; now widespread throughout North and South Islands, but no other islands. **Habitat** Open land from coastal dunes, arable crops and pasture, and alpine grasslands from timberline to upper limit of vegetation at *c.* 2000 m elevation. In UK, brown hares are confined to lowland habitat by a related species, the mountain hare (*L. timidus*), which was never brought to NZ. **Food** Mainly native and introduced grasses;

Young female.

34

Leveret.

also browses alpine shrubs and seeds. **Social behaviour** Mainly solitary, nocturnal. Rests by day in a form (shallow scrape in soil), reingesting; congregates at night only at favourable food sources such as a fresh crop of lucerne. Returns before dawn to form, often via circuitous route to confuse predators. **Reproduction** Breeding season starts soon after winter solstice (21 June); >90% females pregnant by August. Gestation 42 days. Adult females produce 4–5 litters of two young a year until February; mate again immediately after previous birth; annual production almost 10 young/year each. Competition between males for access to oestrus females most intense in September. Males gather around a female, chase each other and have stand-up boxing matches (the southern equivalent of the 'mad March hares' of Europe). Early-born young females can breed at 5 months, in season of own birth. Leverets *c.* 125 g at birth, born fully furred and with eyes open; nursed once or twice a night, grow rapidly; weaned at 1–1.5 kg (*c.* 6 weeks), adult size at 5 months. **Populations** Unlike rabbits, hares never reach huge numbers, because their populations are partly self-limited. They produce many fewer young (*c.* 10/female/year) with high mortality (13% of leverets die per month). Up to half the young surviving to independence leave natal area, and those that survive are socially intolerant as adults. Local numbers seldom exceed 2/ha. Adult mortality rate probably 45–65%/year, so very few live to 8 years old. Hares not affected by the rabbit disease RHD, but have benefited from its effect in reducing numbers of rabbits on lowlands, and also from effective control of ungulates on alpine tussocklands. **Status** Introduced. **Management** None. Damage to human interests slight, control seldom justifiable; minor value as game species.

Rats and mice

Order Rodentia

Almost a quarter of all mammal species are rodents, occupying almost every possible habitat around the world. Most are limited in range and numbers, and are seldom seen. A few have become **commensal**; they have struck up a close relationship with humans, can reach enormous numbers, and have hitch-hiked with us around the world. New Zealand is one of hundreds of previously isolated island groups reached by these unintended and unwelcome passengers, with universally drastic consequences.

Kiore, Polynesian rat *Rattus exulans*

Family Muridae. **Identification** Brown back, grey-white belly; tail shorter or longer than head–body length, thin and with no pale underside; ears cover eyes when pulled forward; hind foot dark on outer edge, rest of foot and toes pale brown; eight nipples. Agile climber; unwilling swimmer; nests on ground. Dental formula I1/1, C0/0, Pm0/0, M3/3 = 16. **Similar species** Ship rat larger (120–160 g), tail much longer than head–body, upper side of hind foot uniform colour usually brown. Norway rat much larger (200–300 g), upper side of hind foot always completely pale, tail much shorter than head–body, ears do not cover eyes when pulled forward. **Size** Smallest rat in NZ. Adult weight 60–80 g; head–body 120–160 mm; tail 140–170 mm; ears 15–20 mm; hind foot 24–31 mm. **NZ range** Arrived with human voyagers from eastern Polynesia, the ancestors of modern Maori, at least by AD 1300. Whether rats were put aboard the double-hulled ocean-going canoes deliberately or by accident, and whether these were the first rats to arrive in NZ, are subjects of continuing debate. DNA evidence suggests multiple colonisations from more than one source. In pre-European times, kiore were widespread throughout mainland and Stewart Island and on 44 other islands; throughout 19th century, drastically reduced on mainland by competition with/predation by Norway rats; in late 20th century, subject to vigorous eradication operations around coast; now confined to parts of Fiordland and Stewart Island plus *c.* 20 other offshore islands. **Habitat** Forest, scrub and grasslands, formerly to at least 1300 m, wherever they can find food and refuge from larger rats and other predators. **Food** Omnivorous. Almost any animal (arthropods, worms, land snails, birds, eggs, lizards) or vegetable (flowers, fruit, seeds, bark, rhizomes) food acceptable. **Social behaviour** Unsociable, nocturnal. Breeding females avoid each other; males avoid females except when mating; family ties brief. **Reproduction** Age and size at maturity vary greatly between populations and years, depending on food supply and numbers. Gestation 19–21 days; litter size 4–7; weaned at *c.* 4 weeks; females can average three litters a season. Well-fed young can mature at 50 g and breed in season of own birth. **Populations** In ideal conditions, when seed and litter invertebrates were abundant and competitors few, kiore used to reach huge numbers, much as feral house mice still do. **Status** Introduced, but much longer ago than other rat species. **Management** Mixed. In pre-European times, kiore did immense damage to the smaller native fauna (frogs, lizards and small birds), and still present a risk on the few forested islands where they remain. Once called 'native rat' by the early European naturalists, because it arrived in New Zealand before they did, but this is incorrect. Nevertheless, regarded as taonga (tribal treasures) by some Maori tribes. DoC recognises and allows for this difference in its management of kiore-inhabited islands. Where differences in cultural values can be managed, eradication programmes have demonstrated recovery of vulnerable species on newly rat-free islands. Benefits include appearance of large, previously unknown species of invertebrates and massive increases in numbers of known ones; increased food for, and improved breeding success of, lizards and tuatara; drastic reduction in nesting losses among seabirds; regeneration of island forests in which recruitment has been prevented by predation on seeds and seedlings; prevention of damage to endangered native wood rose.

Norway rat *Rattus norvegicus*

Family Muridae. **Identification** Stocky body with brown back, grey-white belly; heavy tail clearly shorter than head–body, thick with pale underside; ears do not cover eyes when pulled forward; hind foot always pale on top; 12 nipples. Burrows extensively but rarely climbs; strong swimmer (alternative name is 'water rat'); nests underground. Acutely sensitive to scents, sounds, light and touch; sight poor. Four toes in front, five behind. Dental formula I1/1, C0/0, Pm0/0, M3/3 = 16. **Similar species** Kiore much smaller (60–80 g), tail shorter or longer than head–body, hind foot dark on outer edge, rest of foot and toes pale brown; ears cover eyes when pulled forward. Ship rat smaller (120–160 g), tail much longer than head–body, upper side of hind foot uniform colour usually brown, ears cover eyes when pulled forward. **Size** Largest rat in NZ. Adults 200–300 g, a few old ones to 400 g; ears 14–22 mm, hind foot 30–41 mm. **NZ range** Commonest rat on ships 1700–1850. Arrived during or after James Cook's first visit in 1769, disembarking from rat-infested ships of visiting explorers, whalers and traders. Swarmed throughout mainland until mid-19th century, replacing kiore almost everywhere they met, plus >60 large islands including Chatham and Stewart. After 1850–1900 numbers declined, then disappeared from much of mainland; largest remaining populations are commensal. **Habitat** Rubbish dumps, feed and grain stores, farm buildings (ground floors), pigsties, wharves, ditches and sewers; braided river-beds, swamps, lake shores, sand dunes; remnants survive in some forests, especially along streams. Avoids high elevations on mainland, but ranges to >700 m on Stewart Island. **Food** Omnivorous, including everything humans eat and more. Very careful about tasting new and unfamiliar foods, such as poison baits. Young learn from mother what is safe by taking food from her mouth, and by watching what other rats eat. All native fauna feeding

or nesting on ground are vulnerable. **Social behaviour** Sociable, nocturnal. Social system hierarchical; interactions and home ranges fluid, changeable according to opportunity. **Reproduction** Breed all year; gestation 21–24 days; average of eight kits born at 4–6 g naked, blind; eyes open at 2 weeks, weaned at 4 weeks. Weight at independence 30–40 g, at maturity >85 g; early-born females can breed in season of own birth; growth continues slowly throughout life. **Populations** Where food abundant and other rats/predators few, annual productivity of potentially 20–40 young/female can push numbers to plague proportions, with devastating consequences, e.g. during earliest invasion of any new area. **Status** Introduced. **Management** Major pest. Since *c.* 1985, new technology and visionary planning has enabled eradication of Norway rats from about half

the islands they once colonised, including many considered impossible to clear only 20 years ago, e.g. Kapiti in 1996 (1970 ha), Campbell in 2001 (11,331 ha) and Raoul in 2002 (2938 ha), with wonderful results. Potential value clear by 1986, when rats

Male, swimming.

removed from 170 ha Breaksea Island; skinks recolonised from adjacent rock stacks, and endangered native insects and birds were reintroduced. On Campbell Island the critically endangered local species of snipe sat out the 1840–2001 rat invasion undetected on tiny (19 ha) Jacquemart Island, 1 km offshore, but returned unaided after the rats had gone.

Female eating weta.

Ship rat *Rattus rattus*

Black morph.

Family Muridae. **Identification** Sleek, slender body with three distinct colour phases, all interfertile, varying in proportions around NZ, known by Latin names: *alexandrinus*, brown back, grey belly (rare in most of North Island); *frugivorous*, brown back, white/pale lemon belly (rare in South Island); *rattus*, black back, grey belly (absent from Stewart Island). Tail much longer than head–body, dark all over; ears thin, hairless, 19–26 mm, cover eyes when pulled forward; hind foot 28–38 mm, dark all over, five toes (four in front); 10 nipples. Climbs as well and often as any squirrel, up wires and along thin branches, in ceilings (alternative name is 'roof rat'); rarely burrows or swims; nests mainly in trees. Dental formula I1/1, C0/0, Pm0/0, M3/3 = 16. **Similar species** Kiore much smaller (60–80 g), tail shorter or longer than head–body, hind foot dark on outer edge, rest of foot and toes pale brown. Norway rat much larger (200–300 g), upper side of hind foot always completely pale, tail much shorter than head–body, ears do not cover eyes when pulled forward. **Size** Adults 120–160 g; ears 19–26 mm; hind foot 28–38 mm. **NZ range** Extremely widespread but seldom seen. Commonest rat on ships after 1850. Since then, huge populations established on mainland, Stewart Island and *c.* 60 other islands, replacing Norway rats in all types of forest; in buildings, avoids them by living only in upper levels. **Habitat** Abundant in podocarp-broadleaf forests, regardless of logging history; less so in parks, farms, hedgerows, pine forest; scarce in beech forest except after a heavy seedfall, and in alpine zone. **Food** Omnivorous. All kinds of fruit, seeds, insects, snails, birds, eggs, and probably lizards. Construct feeding platforms up trees which accumulate gnawed seed cases, egg/snail shells, bird bones, insect remains. **Social behaviour** Sociable, nocturnal. Individuals/family groups live evenly dispersed through forests, as dictated to adult females by food supplies; males follow females, travelling up to 700 m a night searching for them.

Frugivorous morph: adults fighting over dead fish.

Home ranges are three-dimensional, including space above ground accessible by climbing, used for foraging and nesting. Neighbours keep in close touch, so residents killed during control operations quickly replaced by immigrants. **Reproduction** Gestation 20–22 days; litters average 5–8, produced *c.* once a month; pups grow rapidly, weaned at *c.* 40 g after 21–28 days, mature by *c.* 3–4 months old. Dark spots on uterus of an adult female indicate number of young produced in her lifetime; average productivity varies with conditions, easily 10–20 young/female/year. Annual mortality rate *c.* 90%; most live <1 year; a few to third year. Breeding normally stops in winter, except when food abundant, as after heavy seedfall. **Populations** Numbers in long-established mixed forest populations average 2–6/ha; much higher on islands (e.g. 25–50/ha on Haulashore Island, Nelson, before 1991 eradication) and during early stages of invasions. Predation by cats and stoats on rats often heavy; effects on rat population depend on replacement rate. **Status** Introduced. **Management** Major pest. Predation by ship rats on native fauna widespread, severe, and continuous in North Island for at least 150 years, and in South Island >100 years; consequences for NZ biodiversity devastating. On mainland, proportion of damage due to rats, as opposed to stoats, ferrets and/or cats, cannot now be separated, but ship rats are much more widespread and much more abundant than any carnivores; effective control or exclusion of ship rats (and possums) has permitted some spectacular conservation benefits for e.g. kokako, robin, tomtit, NZ pigeon, land snails and invertebrates. Island eradications (nine done, 26 to go) continue to expand the number of rat-free refuges for threatened species, although too late for some, e.g. nine (five endemic) species lost from Big South Cape Island in 1960s.

House mouse *Mus musculus*

Female.

Family Muridae. **Identification** Grey-brown back, pale grey or white belly; tail shorter or longer than body, grey-brown all over; ears 12–15 mm, hind foot 15–21 mm; 10–12 nipples. Lives mainly on ground but climbs well; nests in almost any small, dry cavity. Genetic heritage of NZ mice a complex mixture of uncertain history and multiple origins, dominated by western European subspecies plus contributions from north European and Asian stock. Dental formula I1/1, C0/0, Pm0/0, M3/3 = 16. **Similar species** Juvenile rats seldom leave nest until they weigh >30 g; those that do have hind feet longer than 21 mm. No other rodent has a distinct notch on inside of upper incisors. **Size** Adults 15–20 g; tail 80–100 mm; hind foot 15–21 mm. **NZ range** Mice absent from pre-European Polynesia; arrived in NZ only after early 1800s, as stowaways on European ships. Spread throughout mainland from coast to tree line, and to *c.* 50 offshore islands, especially those without Norway rats. **Habitat** In other countries, commensal house mice do live in houses, and field mice are completely different animals. In NZ there are no other kinds of mice, so house mice live both in town and in the country. Habitats include native and exotic forest, scrub, pasture, tussock, crops, sand dunes, gorse and overgrown road verges; also houses, food stores, rubbish tips, haystacks and farm buildings. Prefer thick cover offering escape from predators. **Food** Omnivorous. Insects, molluscs, worms, eggs, fruit, fungi, seeds of native trees (hundreds at a time), totalling *c.* 5 g a day. **Social behaviour** Sociable or solitary, depending on conditions; nocturnal. **Reproduction** Gestation 19–21 days; litter size 5–7; born blind, naked, 1 g; eyes open, fully furred by 14 days; weaned at 20–23 days, *c.* 6 g; mature at *c.* 8 weeks, 10–12 g. Males can be fertile all year but females stop breeding in autumn, except when food abundant. After a heavy seedfall of forest trees, breeding continues over winter and juvenile survival is high, so huge numbers of young mice appear in spring/early summer, providing a vital resource for breeding female stoats. **Populations** Numbers generally limited by shortage of protein food and/or relentless predation; capable of dramatic irruptions after local eradication of rats and in beech mast years. Most mice live <6 months, rarely to 12 months. Predators cannot prevent spring irruptions because mice can easily replace the losses; past the peak, recruitment of young mice ceases and numbers decline even where predators absent. **Status** Introduced. **Management** Pest. On mainland, mice are minor pests compared with rats, cats and stoats, although mice help sustain populations of these more serious predators. Inside pest-proof fences, irruptions of mice cause concern for native invertebrates and lizards; on Antipodes Island, large native beetles scarce but survive on adjacent mouse-free Bollons Island. Eradication of mice more difficult than of rats, so completed only on 14 islands so far.

12-day-old young in nest.

Whales and dolphins

Order Cetacea

Whales and dolphins are superbly specialised, fully aquatic mammals. Yet, because all mammals lived on land at the time the dinosaurs disappeared (65 million years ago), it has always been obvious that cetaceans must be descended from terrestrial ancestors. Some, such as the sperm whale, still retain tiny vestigial hind limbs (see p. 55). The story of this extraordinary transition is now well documented by a beautiful series of amphibious intermediates, preserved as fossils over the last 50 million years.

Two suborders of cetaceans, toothed and non-toothed, have been evolving separately for most of that time, and are now very different. Toothed whales have single blow-holes, and range in size from the 1.4 m Hector's dolphin (small by cetacean standards) to the 15 m sperm whale. The baleen whales have paired blow-holes, and range from the 5 m pygmy right whale to the 30 m blue whale.

Deep-sea and shore-based whaling, unregulated throughout the 1800s, devastated all populations of large whales throughout New Zealand waters. When that became uneconomic, whalers shifted to the Antarctic in 1904, using factory ships that could be independent of shore for long periods. They concentrated first on the biggest species, blue and humpback whales; as those stocks dwindled, they moved on in turn to sei, fin and minke whales.

The last operational shore whaling station in New Zealand closed in 1964; remains of some of its buildings are visible from the inter-island ferries as they pass through Tory Channel. Most pelagic whaling stopped in 1986. The International Whaling Commission (IWC, established 1946) now regulates commercial operations, and in 1994 established a circumpolar Southern Ocean whale sanctuary extending from Antarctica to 40°S, which includes New Zealand waters south of about Wanganui. In addition, New Zealand legislation protects all cetaceans throughout New Zealand territorial waters.

Thousands of cetaceans have stranded on the New Zealand coast since records began around 1880. Baleen whales strand rarely and singly, but toothed whales strand often and in large groups. Rescue operations are well organised and often successful, depending on the extent of injuries to the animals. Swift action is vital, so if you find or suspect a stranding, alert the local DoC office immediately, or call the DoC emergency number, 0800 36 24 68.

Baleen whales

Suborder Mysticeti: baleen whales

Baleen whales feed by swimming into a school of krill (small crustaceans) or fish, taking huge volumes of water into their mouths and straining it out sideways past the baleen plates. This filtering system is very efficient, and allows the baleen whales to reach enormous sizes.

Humpback whale *Megaptera novaeangliae*

Family Balaenopteridae. **Identification** Blackish on body; white under throat, on flippers and under tail flukes. Flippers very large (5 m, >25% body length), scalloped on leading edge, can be smacked on the surface to make a loud noise. Sometimes leap clear of water, returning with enormous splash. Rough knobbly skin on head usually encrusted with barnacles. Shows tail flukes when diving. **Similar species** No other large whale has white underside to tail flukes and disproportionately large flippers. **Size** Adults average 15 m, 30–40 tonnes; calves 4.5 m, 1.3 tonnes at birth. **NZ range** Coastal. Migrates between Antarctica and breeding grounds north of NZ; travels north via east coast in autumn and returns past west coast in spring. **Food** Krill, schooling fish. Humpbacks concentrate schools of prey with a 'bubble net'. They create the net by forcing air out of the blow-hole while swimming upwards, eventually surfacing through the centre of the school with mouth wide open. **Social behaviour** Social groups communicate using long, variable songs, each song unique to one group. Songs well known from recordings, but real is function unknown. **Reproduction** Mature by 10 years; gestation 11–12 months; calves nurse for 12 months, until 8 m long. **Populations** Numbers drastically reduced during 1950s; now fewer than 2000 in whole southern hemisphere, of which <300 migrate past New Zealand. Sightings in Cook Strait reduced from 500 to 23 over 10 years to 1963, but now recovering. **Status** Native. **Management** Protected since 1963. IUCN category Vulnerable.

© SeaPics.com

45

Blue whale *Balaenoptera musculus*

© SeaPics.com

Family Balaenopteridae. **Identification** Blue-grey body with pale patches; dorsal fin small, near tail; throat grooves, baleen plates black. Throat grooves extend *c.* 60% of body. Does not show tail flukes when diving. There is a complete skeleton in the Canterbury Museum. **Similar species** Right whales have bowheads and two short throat grooves or none (southern right whale has horny growths on head, pygmy right whale has smooth head); throat grooves on sei and minke whales end before navel (baleen plates in sei are black, yellow in minke); in other large whales with throat grooves extending past navel, humpback has flippers >25% body length, Bryde's whale has three ridges on top of head, fin whale two ridges cross flattened top of head. **Size** Adults 25–30 m long, weight 80–130 tonnes (females generally larger than males); calves 7 m long and 7 tonnes at birth. **NZ range** Pelagic, so rarely strands or seen from land. Migrates from Antarctic to warmer waters for breeding season when ice closes feeding areas in March. **Food** Feeds mainly on krill, especially in areas of upwelling around edge of polar ice during feeding season December–February. Can dive deep and stay down half an hour; on surfacing, can blow spray up to 12 m high. **Reproduction** Calves born in tropical waters during non-feeding season. Gestation 11–12 months; calves fed on abundant (600 L/day) rich milk, double birth weight in a week. Weaned at *c.* 7 months old, 15 m long; females breed every third year. **Populations** Main target species of Antarctic whaling fleets 1925–38; 350,000 killed from 1904 to 1967, including 30,000 in 1930–31 alone. Total surviving population <500. **Status** Native. **Management** Protected since 1967. IUCN category Endangered.

Fin whale *Balaenoptera physalus*

Family Balaenopteridae. **Identification** Dark grey body, white below and on right side of head; head flattened on top; dorsal fin 0.6 m tall, set well back; flippers small. Seldom shows flukes when diving. There are skeletons in Otago Museum, Dunedin, and in Te Papa, Wellington. **Similar species** No other whale has asymmetrical head colouring. **Size** Average 21 m in males, 25 m in females; weight *c.* 35–45 tonnes; calves 6.5 m, 3.5 tonnes at birth. **NZ range** Main migration route well offshore, so seldom seen. **Food** Generalist feeder on krill, fish, squid. Often sweeps prey at surface, but can dive to >250 m. **Social behaviour** Normal social unit 6–15, including adult males. **Reproduction** Matures at 6–7 years; migrates to and mates in warm tropical waters during southern winter, young born in same area the following year. Lactation 6 months, ending when calf has doubled its length to 12 m. **Populations** Can swim at >40 kph, so could easily escape whalers until invention of motor-powered catchers. Then, >700,000 caught in southern hemisphere alone 1904–79. Present total population *c.* 70,000–80,000. **Status** Native. **Management** Protected since 1970s. IUCN category Vulnerable.

Sei whale *Balaenoptera borealis*

© SeaPics.com

Family Balaenopteridae. **Identification** Similar to fin whale, but steely grey and no asymmetry of head colour; dorsal fin larger than in blue whale, and set further forward; many conspicuous throat grooves ending before navel; pectoral fins small. Baleen plates black, with fine white bristles. Does not show tail flukes when diving. **Similar species** Right whales have bowheads and two short throat grooves or none (southern right whale has horny growths on head and no dorsal fin, pygmy right whale has smooth head); minke whale also has conspicuous throat grooves ending before navel but yellow baleen plates; other large whales have many conspicuous throat grooves extending past navel (flippers >25% body length in humpback, three ridges on top of head in Bryde's whale, two ridges in fin whale, no ridges in blue whale). **Size** Adults 15–16 m, 12–15 tonnes; calves 4.5 m, 900 kg at birth. **NZ range** Pelagic or coastal outside 100 m line. No regular migration route past NZ. **Food** Fish, crustaceans, squid, plankton, whatever is abundant and easily skimmed from the surface, amounting to 900 kg of assorted prey per day. **Social behaviour** Lives in family groups, aggregating only at rich feeding sites. Forms firm pair bonds, may even be monogamous. **Populations** Gestation plus lactation total 18 months, so females can breed every other year. Frequently killed by Antarctic whalers in mid-1960s in place of blue whales (protected) and fin whales (depleted). Southern population now >50,000. **Status** Native. **Management** Protected since 1970s. IUCN category Endangered.

Antarctic minke whale *Balaenoptera bonaerensis*

Family Balaenopteridae. **Identification** Bluish grey above, lighter below. Rostrum narrow, pointed; dorsal fin set well back; flippers pointed, often marked with a variable white patch; conspicuous throat grooves ending before navel; baleen plates yellow with white fringe. Does not show tail flukes when diving. **Similar species** Common minke whale (*B. acutorostrata*) confined to northern hemisphere. An as yet unnamed but highly recognisable subspecies of *acutorostrata*, the dwarf minke whale (illustrated), is found in warmer waters in NZ. It reaches only 7 m in length and has a conspicuous white spot on the flippers. Right whales have two short throat grooves or none (southern right whale has horny growths on head, pygmy right whale has smooth head); sei whale also has throat grooves ending before navel but black baleen plates; other large whales have many conspicuous throat grooves extending past navel (flippers >25% body length in humpback, three ridges on top of head in Bryde's whale, two ridges in fin whale, no ridges in blue whale). **Size** Adults average 8–9 m, 6–7 tonnes; calves *c.* 3 m, 450 kg at birth. **NZ range** More coastal than larger baleen whales; sighted in small pods around NZ, occasionally strands (>15 successfully refloated). **Food** Fish, squid and krill. **Populations** Removal of competition for krill from blue whales has benefited minke; numbers recovering well. Can sustain a substantial harvest (e.g. 98,000 in Antarctic between 1957/58 and 1986/87); present southern population >200,000. **Status** Native. **Management** Since 1986, IWC has permitted Japanese whalers to take 250–300 southern minke per year for research. IUCN category Data Deficient.

© SeaPics.com

Dwarf minke whale.

Bryde's whale *Balaenoptera brydei*

Family Balaenopteridae. **Identification** Similar to sei whale, but with smaller dorsal fin and three ridges along top of head; throat grooves run along belly to navel; dark grey above, paler below. Baleen plates grey to black. Does not show tail flukes when diving. **Similar species** Right whales have bowheads and two short throat grooves or none (southern right whale has horny growths on head, pygmy right whale has smooth head); sei and minke whales also have conspicuous throat grooves ending before navel but baleen plates in sei are black with fine white bristles, yellow in minke; other large whales have many conspicuous throat grooves extending past navel (flippers >25% body length in humpback, two ridges on top of head in fin whale, no ridges in blue whale). **Size** Adults 12–16 m, average 12 tonnes; calves 4 m, 900 kg at birth. **NZ range** Core range in inshore warm temperate waters; in NZ seen mainly north of East Cape and particularly in Hauraki Gulf. **Food** Mainly fish, e.g. saury, pilchards, anchovy, jack mackerel, but also krill. No clear separation between feeding and breeding seasons, as in larger baleen whales. **Social behaviour** Live in loose social groups of 3–6; breed late winter/early spring. **Populations** NZ population probably <200, belonging to one of three closely related but poorly defined species totalling *c.* 80,000. **Status** Vagrant. **Management** None. IUCN category Data Deficient.

Southern right whale *Eubalaena australis*

Family Balaenidae. **Identification** Body rotund and almost entirely black except for white blotches on chin; no dorsal fin; head very large (*c.* 25% of body) with arched upper jaw ('bowhead') supporting baleen plates >2 m long; no throat grooves; various lumps or calluses on head, usually infested with barnacles and parasites. Slow-moving, rich in oil and long baleen, floats when dead, hence it was the 'right' whale for early whalers to hunt in rowing boats. Calves often much paler than adults, or even white. Shows tail flukes when diving. Skeleton easily identified from high arched upper jaw and fused cervical vertebrae. **Similar species** No other large whale lacks a dorsal fin. Dorsal fin provides stability to faster-swimming cetaceans, but right whales swim too slowly to need one. **Size** Adults average 15 m, 55 tonnes; calves 5–6 m at birth. **NZ range** Prefers shallow water, and well adapted to it, so rarely strands. Adults and calves are regular visitors to NZ waters, especially the east coast and Auckland and Campbell Islands in winter and spring. **Food** Collects food at surface by cruising through shoaling plankton with mouth open, closing it every so often to strain material through baleen plates. **Social behaviour** Weaned calves stay close to mother for 2–3 years. Family bonds strong; mothers protect young even from harpoons. **Reproduction** Mating starts on the NZ coast in early spring, and is boisterous and competitive (testes of adult males reach 900 kg each, the largest in the animal kingdom). Females mature at *c.* 10 years old; gestation 9–10 months; calf born during winter in a shallow bay, suckles 12 months. **Populations** Hunted almost to extinction, now slowly recovering. In 1992 RNZAF found and photographed a group of 70 right whales plus a white calf at the Auckland Islands. Southern population about 3000. **Status** Native. **Management** Protected. IUCN category Low Risk, depending on conservation measures.

Pygmy right whale *Caperea marginata*

Family Balaenidae. **Identification** Black or dark grey above, light grey to white beneath; baleen plates white with black margins, contrasting with head colour when mouth open. Smallest of the bowhead whales; no calluses on head; two deep throat grooves but no multiple pleats. Pushes snout out of water to breathe rather than spouting; sinks without showing fin or flukes; never leaps or splashes. **Similar species** No other bowhead whale has a dorsal fin. **Size** Adults average 5 m, 4.5 tonnes; calves 2 m at birth. **NZ range** Seldom seen at sea; occasionally stranded in NZ. **Status** Vagrant. **Management** None. IUCN category Data Deficient.

Toothed whales

Suborder Odontoceti: toothed whales

The toothed whales are fast-swimming and active hunters. They lack vocal cords, but use a variety of clicks generated by the single blow-hole to create a stream of sound signals, which serve in communication and echolocation. They have large brains and a 'melon' in the head, used as a lens to focus sound waves. Some species have more than 100 similar peg-like teeth, some have a few, rather bizarre-shaped teeth. Those with few teeth are more likely to use them for display rather than for feeding.

Family Ziphiidae: beaked whales

All whales in this family are medium-sized, with a pointed beak and few teeth. The single blow-hole is crescent-shaped. Other species from NZ waters not shown here include Cuvier's beaked whale (*Ziphius cavirostris*), Arnoux's beaked whale (*Beradius arnuxii*), Shepherd's beaked whale (*Tasmacetus shepherdi*), dense-beaked whale (*Mesoplodon densirostris*), Andrew's beaked whale (*M. bowdoini*), Peruvian beaked whale (*M. peruvianus*), Hector's beaked whale (*M. hectori*), ginkgo-toothed whale (*M. ginkgodens*) and spade-toothed whale (*M traversii*). They are typically seen only as strandings, probably live in canyons and eat mainly squid.

Gray's beaked whale *Mesoplodon grayi*

Family Ziphiidae. **Identification** Deep grey to black, paler grey below; jaws, throat white; paler spots, scars, scattered over whole body. Both sexes have only one pair of teeth on the lower jaw, which are triangular, laterally flattened, with a terminal point. The upper jaw contains 17–22 small teeth. Head with a small bulge in front of blow-hole; prominent throat grooves; slender body with short wide flippers. Dorsal fin pointed. **Similar species** Several similar species of beaked whale difficult to tell apart. **Size** Adults 3–4 m, *c.* 1 tonne. **NZ range** Best known from strandings in NZ (first discovered after 25 stranded on Chatham Islands in 1874; >20 other cases since). Sociable. **Status** Native. **Management** None.

Strap-toothed whale *Mesoplodon layardi*

Family Ziphiidae. **Identification** Long body laterally compressed, dark grey above, paler below, some with a pale patch on top of head and around vent; long slender beak, mostly white. Small flippers and dorsal fin. In males only, a single pair of large, strap-shaped teeth (30 cm long, 4–5 cm wide) protrude backwards at 45° angle from lower jaw, curve over upper jaw, eventually limit opening of mouth. **Similar species** Gray's beaked whale has short triangular teeth. **Size** Adults 5–7 m, *c.* 1–2 tonnes. **NZ range** Restricted to southern hemisphere; may turn up anywhere around NZ coast. **Status** Native. **Management** None.

Family Physeteridae: sperm whales

The three members of this family have in common a spermaceti organ and no visible teeth in the upper jaw, and all use echolocation for hunting and social communication. Two of them, the pygmy and dwarf sperm whales, are different in many other respects and should probably be moved to a family of their own. The family name comes from the (wrong) idea of early whalers that the spermaceti organ (a reservoir of clear liquid that sets to solid wax on cooling) was connected with reproduction. It is more likely to be a device to adjust buoyancy during deep dives.

Sperm whale *Physeter macrocephalus*

© SeaPics.com

Family Physeteridae. **Identification** Largest of all toothed whales; huge square head (>35% of body) with terminal blow-hole on left side and relatively small, underslung toothed lower jaw; teeth 20 cm long, 10 cm diameter, with no enamel, appear only after age 10 (teeth of upper jaw seldom erupt). No true dorsal fin, but a series of low humps or ridges along spine; very broad flukes but small flippers; defleshed skeletons reveal tiny vestigial hind limbs. Grey, corrugated hide with a few white patches, becoming larger with age; old males (as in the mythical 'Moby Dick') can become all white. Flukes dark underneath, always show on diving. **Similar species** Flukes of humpback are white underneath. Pygmy and dwarf sperm whales have much smaller bodies, teeth up to 2 cm diameter, rounded heads. **Size** Adults average 11–15 m, 20–35 tonnes (males larger); calves 4 m at birth. **NZ range** Females and calves confined to warm latitudes; males travel to high latitudes in summer to feed, alone or in casual bachelor herds, returning in winter. Mass strandings (usually females and calves) recorded near Gisborne in 1970 (59 animals) and at Muriwai in 1974 (72 animals). **Food** Adults specialise in preying on deep-water giant squid, and frequently dive to below 1000 m to find them. Head, jaw of most adult sperm whales patterned with circular scars up to 12–15 cm diameter, made by suckers on squid tentacles. Other food items recorded include 4 m sharks, skate, fish; even boots, buckets and plastic bags. During deep dives, cold water used to cool spermaceti organ and increase its density, providing neutral buoyancy at any depth. **Social behaviour** Males >25 years old compete for access to females; successful males hold their harem until following spring. Females and calves live in large, strongly bonded pods, keeping in contact by echolocation (each produces individually distinct clicks). Mass strandings seem to be initiated by a single beached individual whose distress calls bring the others in. The rest of the pod can be prevented from stranding if the injured animal is quickly silenced. Males less strongly bonded, so less likely to strand en masse; they are not aggressive but, if rammed accidentally while sleeping at the surface, may turn and attack even a large ship. **Reproduction** Gestation 14–16 months, lactation 12–24 months; resting phase 9 months, so entire breeding cycle can be 4 years. Females help each other when giving birth and to defend calves from attack by killer whales. **Populations** During the 19th and 20th centuries, whalers took advantage of the social bonding among sperm whales to kill thousands a year (the American whaling fleet had 729 ships by 1850; with more advanced technology, 30,000 sperm whales killed in 1963 alone). Southern population probably >100,000. Still common enough around Cook Strait to support commercial whale-watching trips from Kaikoura. **Status** Native. **Management** IUCN category Data Deficient.

Pygmy sperm whale *Kogia breviceps*

Family Physeteridae. **Identification** Grey to pinkish, even purplish, seldom scarred; white bracket mark ('false gill') behind eye, plus white spot forward of eye. Bulbous nose filled with spermaceti comprises only about 15% of body; blow-hole on top left of head. Short broad flippers well forward; curved dorsal fin. Lower jaw has 12–16 pairs of recurved, sharp teeth. **Similar species** Sperm whale has much larger body with square head, teeth up to 10 cm diameter; dwarf sperm whale (*Kogia simus*) has no white spot in front of eye. **Size** Adults average 3 m, 350 kg; calves 1 m, 55 kg at birth. **NZ range** Often strands on NZ beaches (>250 known cases), usually alone or in mother-calf pairs. Nothing known of population numbers. **Status** Vagrant. **Management** IUCN category Data Deficient.

Family Globiocephalidae: killer and pilot whales

Some authorities place the pilot and killer whales among the true dolphins (Delphinidae), but others argue that their differences (blunt heads with no beaks, and fewer teeth) justify returning them to the separate family set up for them in 1866 (Globiocephalidae). Males are usually conspicuously larger than females; all use echolocation for hunting and social communication.

Killer whale/orca *Orcinus orca*

Family Globiocephalidae. **Identification** Unmistakable black and white markings, individually variable; blunt, powerful head with 11–13 pairs of large conical teeth in each jaw, oval in section; large rounded flippers; tall dorsal fin (to 1.9 m and straight in males, 0.9 m and slightly hooked in females). Once believed to be dangerously aggressive (Linnaeus' original name meant 'demon dolphin') but no deliberate fatal attacks on humans ever recorded. **Similar species** No other cetaceans have obvious black and white

Adult female.

markings and rounded flippers. **Size** Adults average 7–8 m, weight 4–6 tonnes; calves *c.* 2 m at birth. **NZ range** Commonly seen in NZ coastal waters, even inside enclosed areas including Wellington Harbour and Bay of Islands, but may not be a big population, perhaps just a few hundred circulating around the coasts. Mass strandings rare (largest 17 at Paraparaumu, 1955; 11 on Chatham Islands, 1981). **Food** Most dives short, shallow; hunting is strongly cooperative. Prey includes almost anything they can handle: fish, squid, rays, sharks, seals, sea lions, seabirds, small dolphins and young baleen whales. **Social behaviour** Strongly social. Extended family pods including both sexes, all ages, usually 2–40 strong. **Reproduction** Gestation 12 months; calves born in shallow water in autumn/early winter. **Status** Native. **Management** IUCN category Low Risk.

Pod of females in Antarctic waters.

Barbara Todd

Adult male.

59

False killer whale *Pseudorca crassidens*

© SeaPics.com

Family Globiocephalidae. **Identification** Slim body entirely black; rounded snout with 8–10 pairs large teeth in both upper and lower jaws, circular in section; flippers slightly curved on leading edge; dorsal fin sharply raked. Fast-swimming for their size, and are the largest whales capable of bow-wave riding, but are not fast enough to sustain it if ship is doing >25 kph. **Similar species** Killer whale has prominent white markings, teeth oval in section, rounded flippers, larger and more upright dorsal fin; both species of pilot whales have more distinctly curved flippers. **Size** Adults 4–5 m, 1–2 tonnes; calves 1.5 m, 80 kg at birth. **NZ range** Coastal waters anywhere. **Food** Squid and fish, including fast-swimming species such as bonito and tuna. **Social behaviour** Travels in pods hundreds strong, leading to some very large mass strandings (231 at Manukau in 1978). Pod members communicate with each other by diverse, piercing whistles audible to humans. **Reproduction** Gestation 15 months, mature at 8–12 years, breed any time of year. **Status** Native. **Management** IUCN category Data Deficient.

Long-finned pilot whale *Globiocephala melas*

Family Globiocephalidae. **Identification** Large bulbous head, blunt nose, upward-sloping mouth with 8–11 pairs of teeth in each jaw. Body black (hence also called 'blackfish') except for patches of white behind dorsal fin, and of pinkish-grey forward of flippers, extending as a thin band along midline of otherwise grey belly. Dorsal fin curved, broad at base; flippers long (18–27% of body length), sickle-shaped. **Similar species** Killer whale has prominent white markings and round flippers; false killer whale entirely black, flippers only slightly curved. The most similar species, the short-finned pilot whale (*Globiocephala macrorhynchus*) was recognised as a separate species only in 1977; it has shorter flippers (<18% body length) and fewer teeth (7–10 pairs). **Size** Adults 5–6 m, 2–4 tonnes; calves 1.8 m, 100 kg at birth. **NZ range** Commonly stranded around NZ coast, usually in large groups. In one sample of 120 mass strandings, average group size was 78, but several were 200+. Some of these could have been short-finned pilot whales. **Food** Mixed squid and fish. Most dives only to 30–60 m, but easily go much deeper, even to 1000 m. **Social behaviour** Social cohesion extremely strong, maintained by continuous stream of varied sound signals, so whatever happens to any one of a large group usually affects them all. Travelling groups move in line astern or along a broad front with mature males leading; loafing groups sleep in close contact. Strandings of such large groups often dramatic, since surviving or refloated individuals will not leave beached pod-mates while they still live. At sea, groups are hierarchical and polygamous. **Reproduction** Mature at *c.* 6 years, females breed then but males not till *c.* 12 years; gestation 16 months, births in all seasons; lactation *c.* 20 months. **Status** Native. **Management** IUCN category Data Deficient.

Dolphins

Family Delphinidae: true dolphins

The classic dolphins are a group of small (<4 m), agile, fast-swimming cetaceans with slender, streamlined bodies, large dorsal fins and thin pointed snouts.

Dusky dolphin *Lagenorhynchus obscurus*

Family Delphinidae. **Identification** Blue-black on back, with broad white stripes, tail white below; snout dark with almost no beak; flippers grey; dorsal fin dark in front, trailing edge grey. Jaw with 29–35 pairs of small (3 mm diameter) teeth in each jaw. Spectacular natural acrobats, leaping and somersaulting spontaneously at sea, and (formerly) on command at Marineland, Napier. Capable of bow-riding vessels moving at 35 kph, especially small boats. **Similar species** Risso's dolphin has total of 6–14 teeth in lower jaw only; bottlenose and Hector's dolphins have teeth in both jaws totalling more than 80 but less than 100 (bottlenose dolphin has short beak with lower jaw longer than upper; Hector's dolphin has almost no beak and a rounded dorsal fin); southern right whale and common dolphins have more than 80 teeth in each jaw (southern right whale dolphin has no dorsal fin; common and hourglass dolphins both have hourglass pattern on flank but common has >112 teeth). **Size** Adults 1.8–2.1 m, 115 kg; calves 60 cm, 5 kg at birth. **NZ range** Common from Hawke's Bay to Campbell Island, rare further north. **Food** Fish, squid and various bottom-dwelling prey. **Reproduction** Gestation about 9 months; calves born mid winter in northern parts of range. **Status** Native. **Management** IUCN category Data Deficient.

© SeaPics.com

Hourglass dolphin *Lagenorhynchus cruciger*

Family Delphinidae. **Identification** Bold black and white pattern on flanks, comprising two large white patches linked by narrow black band; snout black with short beak; belly white, flippers and dorsal fin black, tailstock keeled. Jaw with 28 pairs of small (3 mm diameter) teeth in each jaw (total 112). Avid bow-riders. **Similar species** No other dolphin has such a striking cross-shaped black and white colouration, visible from afar, and is consistently found as far south as the Antarctic Convergence. **Size** Smallest dolphin of this group. Adults 1.6–1.8 m, 100 kg; calves 50 cm, 4 kg at birth. **NZ range** Largely confined to

© SeaPics.com

cold waters of Southern Ocean, all the way to edge of the ice pack. Seldom strands. Almost nothing known of its natural history. **Status** Native. **Management** IUCN category Data Deficient.

Southern right whale dolphin *Lissodelphis peronii*

© SeaPics.com

Family Delphinidae. **Identification** Back, tail black; snout, throat, flippers, belly, underside of flukes all white; 88–98 small pointed teeth in both upper and lower jaws. Named for total lack of dorsal fin (as in right whale); instead, right whale dolphins achieve stability from flattened body with flippers placed at extreme widest point. **Similar species** No other dolphin lacks a dorsal fin. **Size** Adults average 1.8 m, 60 kg. **NZ range** Usually stays well offshore, feeding on fish and squid in groups of up to 1000. In NZ, 75 stranded on Chatham Islands in 1988. **Status** Native. **Management** IUCN category Data Deficient.

Hector's dolphin *Cephalorhynchus hectori hectori*

Family Delphinidae. **Identification.** Grey back, black cheeks and snout, pale grey to white cap, white throat, belly, black flippers, under tail and flukes. Body rotund, pointed head with no beak; 27–32 pairs of teeth in upper and lower jaws. Dorsal fin and flippers smoothly rounded. **Similar species** Maui's dolphin looks and behaves almost the same, but is a genetically distinct subspecies confined to North Island waters. No other dolphins have a rounded dorsal fin. **Size** Adults average 1.4 m, 40 kg. **NZ range** Close to shore and in estuaries around South Island coasts. **Food** Shallow water/bottom-living fish, cuttlefish, shrimps, crustaceans; attracted to and very vulnerable to entanglement in set nets. **Social behaviour** Live in small sociable groups of 2–10. Friendly to small boats and swimmers. **Populations** Genetically distinct populations of Hector's dolphins on east, west and north-west coasts of South Island, all distinct from Maui's. About 7000 left. **Status** Endemic. **Management** IUCN category Endangered. Marine sanctuaries, where set-netting prohibited, declared especially for these dolphins, but total numbers still declining.

© SeaPics.com

Maui's dolphin *Cephalorhynchus hectori maui*

Family Delphinidae. **Identification** Grey back, black cheeks and snout, pale grey to white cap, white throat, belly, black flippers, under tail and flukes. Body rotund, pointed head with no beak; 27–32 pairs of teeth in upper and lower jaws. Dorsal fin and flippers smoothly rounded. **Similar species** Maui's dolphin is a genetically distinct subspecies of Hector's dolphin, which looks and behaves almost the same, but is confined to South Island waters. No other dolphins have a rounded dorsal fin. **NZ range** Close to shore and in estuaries along west coast of North Island, never visits South Island. The Maui's and Hector's dolphin populations must have been geographically separated for a very long time. **Reproduction** Females do not reach breeding age until age 7–9, then have only one calf every 2–4 years. **Populations** Only about 100–110 Maui's dolphins are left, and they cannot withstand any accidental mortality in fishing nets. Potential recovery rate extremely slow. **Status** Endemic. **Management** IUCN category Critically Endangered. Set-netting is banned within 4 nautical miles of the coasts throughout Maui's core range, from Maunganui Bluff to Pariokariwa Point. In addition, all set-netting is banned in the Manukau Harbour entrance west of Puponga Point (Cornwallis) to a point 0.5 nm north of Kauri Point (eastern end of Big Bay), and then to Kauri Point. A proposal for a marine mammal sanctuary to cover Maui's entire range from Maunganui Bluff to Cape Egmont, in all waters less than 100 m deep, is proposed but not yet agreed.

Risso's dolphin *Grampus griseus*

Family Delphinidae. **Identification** Body grey above, paler below, invariably with multiple pale scars especially forward of the dorsal fin; becoming almost white with age. Head blunt, bulbous with a deep median crease; flippers long, pointed; dorsal fin tall (50 cm); 6–14 teeth only at front end of lower jaw. **Similar species** No other dolphin has a median crease on top of head. **Size** Adults average 3 m, 300 kg; calves 1.5 m at birth. **NZ range** Mostly tropical; uncommon in NZ; few stranding records. 'Pelorus Jack', one of the most famous dolphins in NZ history, belonged to this species. Between 1888 and 1912, Jack regularly rode the bow waves of steamers passing the entrance of Pelorus Sound, and accompanied them to Admiralty Bay. He even had his own protection order,

© SeaPics.com

signed by the NZ Colonial Governor in 1904. By the time he disappeared, his size (*c.* 3.7 m, near maximum), and colour (pale to white) confirmed his age (at least 34), a good record for a dolphin. **Food** Mainly squid. **Populations** Abundant, in social groups of 3–30 especially in warmer waters. **Status** Vagrant. **Management** IUCN category Data Deficient.

Short-beaked common dolphin *Delphinus delphis*

Family Delphinidae. **Identification** Distinct 'hour-glass' colour pattern on flanks; dark above, pale below; tall dark dorsal fin; pale frontal stripe crosses dark head above dark eye spot and beak; tip of beak black; dark stripe crosses white area below chin; flippers dark to grey. Teeth 40–55 pairs, small (3 mm diameter) in upper and lower jaws. **Similar species** Risso's dolphin has total of 60–80 teeth in lower jaw only; bottlenose, dusky and Hector's dolphins have teeth in both jaws totalling more than 80 but less than 100 (bottlenose dolphin has short beak with lower jaw longer than upper; dusky dolphin has a short beak and a pointed dorsal fin; Hector's dolphin has almost no beak and a rounded dorsal fin); hourglass dolphin has only 112 teeth in total; southern right whale dolphin has no dorsal fin. **Size** Adults average 2 m, 80 kg; calves 90 cm at birth. **NZ range**

Common in coastal waters all round NZ, often in large pods of over 200 animals. Naturally playful, both at sea (often seen bow-riding regardless of boat speed, rolling sideways to squint up at humans); one survives at Marineland, Napier. Strandings of single animals often recorded, but few large groups. **Food** Squid, schooling fish (sardines, anchovy), and crabs. **Social behaviour** Groups commonly 20–200+, formerly thousands, segregated by age and sex, each with an internal dominance hierarchy. Group members practise remarkable but well-documented mutual assistance (supporting injured individuals, cooperative hunting or defence against sharks). **Reproduction** Gestation 10–11 months; females produce calves every second year. **Status** Native. **Management** IUCN category Low Risk.

67

Bottlenose dolphin *Tursiops truncatus*

Family Delphinidae. **Identification** Light grey shading to pinkish-white; short strong beak with 21–29 pairs of large (6 mm diameter) teeth in both jaws; lower jaw protrudes beyond upper; corner of mouth curves upwards in a permanent 'grin'; tall dorsal fin curves backwards. **Similar species** Risso's dolphin has total of 6–14 teeth in lower jaw only; dusky and Hector's dolphins have teeth in both jaws totalling more than 80 but less than 100 (dusky dolphin has a short beak and a pointed dorsal fin; Hector's dolphin has almost no beak and a rounded dorsal fin); southern right whale dolphin and common dolphin have more than 80 teeth in each jaw (southern right whale dolphin has no dorsal fin; common and hourglass dolphins both have hourglass pattern on flank but common has >112 teeth). **Size** Adults average 3 m, 200 kg; calves 1 m, 32 kg at birth. **NZ range** Common near shore, in small groups of up to 30 animals. Friendly and often willing to cooperate with people, including the famous 'Opo' (a female bottlenose who regularly mingled with swimmers at Opononi in summer 1955–56; a memorial to her now stands outside the local pub). Main objective of dolphin-watching cruises in harbours north of Hauraki Gulf. **Food** Broad diet includes any inshore bottom-dwelling fish, or crabs. May follow trawlers for discards, but also hunt cooperatively. **Social behaviour** Quick to learn, accurate mimic of both other animals and humans, willing to adapt to life in a pool, easily studied. Courtship behaviour elaborate. Cooperative actions and complex communication suggest high intelligence. Natural acrobats and bow-wave riders. **Reproduction** Gestation 12 months; births attended by 'midwives', who wait as calf emerges tail first and carry it to surface to breathe; lactation lasts a year. With calving intervals of 2 years, females can expect to produce *c.* 8 calves in a lifetime. **Status** Native. **Management** IUCN category Data Deficient.

Carnivores

Order Carnivora: carnivores

More than 50 million years ago the ancestors of the modern carnivores split into two main lineages, which have continued to evolve separately ever since. One, the dog branch or canoids, includes eight families of living species, and the other, the cat branch or feloids, has four families. Almost all true carnivores eat meat, so all have one pair of stabbing canine teeth at the front of the mouth, for grabbing fleeing prey, and one pair of slicing carnassial teeth at the corners of the mouth, for shearing off chunks of meat and bone from a carcase. Hunting living prey requires intelligence and keen senses, which all true carnivores demonstrate very well.

In New Zealand, members of the two canoid families Otariidae and Phocidae (the eared and earless seals, respectively) form the largest single group of native land-breeding mammals. In addition, we have three introduced members of another canoid family, the Mustelidae (stoat, weasel and ferret), and a single representative of the feloids, the house cat. Domestic dogs, both Polynesian and European, have accompanied their human masters all around the islands but have no surviving independent feral populations, so are not included here.

Fur seals and sea lions

Family Otariidae: fur seals and sea lions

The fur seals and sea lions have sleek, streamlined bodies, small external ears and long whiskers. They are beautifully agile in water, but they can also move pretty fast on land. They support their weight mainly on their large fore flippers, and climb remarkably well across rocks, using their hind flippers turned forward like back feet. Males compete fiercely for breeding rights, so are much larger than females. Haul-out (resting) sites on land are used most often in winter and spring; rookeries (breeding sites) from November to January. Males and females aggregate only once a year, so females mate again immediately after giving birth. After fertilisation, there is a period of **delayed implantation**; active gestation resumes in time for the foetus to reach full term by next pupping season.

During the peak of sealing (1810–30) all mainland and most accessible southern populations of eared seals were practically exterminated by uncontrolled slaughter. At least 7 million seals were killed by 1833. Commercial harvest was less economic after 1830; closed seasons were imposed 1875; all sealing stopped in 1916.

Male New Zealand fur seal.

New Zealand fur seal *Arctocephalus forsteri*

Male.

Family Otariidae. **Identification** Dark grey-brown in both sexes, males with massive thick necks and heavy mane; pups black to dark brown. Pointed snout with luxuriant whiskers, large dark eyes with no tear duct (fur below eye constantly wet); dense underfur. Senses of hearing and smell more acute than sight. Dental formula I3/2, C 1/1, Pm 4/4, M 2/1 = 36. **Similar species** Subantarctic fur seal has yellow face and chest; NZ sea lion much larger, females grey to white; all true seals lack external ears. **Size** Adult males average 125 kg, females 40 kg; pups 5–6 kg at birth. **NZ range** Virtually all subantarctic islands have breeding sites that have been used for decades. Many new haul-out sites and rookeries have appeared around mainland coasts in the last 20 years, mostly in South Island but now also (after a long absence) southern North Island. **Habitat** Coastal, plus a limited range out to sea. Favours exposed rocky coasts with shallow pools for adults cooling off and pups learning to swim. **Food** Squid, octopus, fish, penguins. **Social behaviour** Males come ashore first, establish territories and defend them against rival males by vigorous chest-pushing or face-slashing contests, if necessary for weeks at a time without eating. Females choose the best territories to produce their pups, and afterwards mate with the territory owner. Some males collect several females, others none; challenges to the haves by the have-nots continue all season, until the end of birthing/mating in January, when the exhausted males return to sea. **Reproduction** Females mature at 4–6 years; receptive for only *c.* 24 hours in December/January; implantation of embryo delayed until April–May; active gestation 7 months. Pups born fully furred and with eyes open; mothers and pups learn each other's

Female and pup.

scent immediately and thereafter reject all others. Mother suckles pup between gradually lengthening foraging trips until September. Can live for 15–20 years. **Populations** Mainland breeding groups hunted for meat by Maori; all populations devastated by European sealers 1792–1830; now steadily recovering. Current total at least 100,000, plus *c.* 40,000 in Australia. **Status** Native. **Management** Protected in 1916, but many still drown in trawl nets (estimated >1000 a year 1989–98).

90-day-old pup.

71

Subantarctic fur seal *Arctocephalus tropicalis*

Male.

Family Otariidae. **Identification** Dark-grey-brown on back, distinctive bright yellow to cream face and chest; males with massive thick necks and heavy mane, topped with a prominent crest, erected when agitated; in all other respects similar to NZ fur seal. **Similar species** NZ fur seal has no yellow markings; NZ sea lion much larger, females grey to white; all true seals lack external ears. **Size** Adult males average 130 kg, females 35 kg; pups 4 kg at birth. **NZ range** Mostly (but still only occasionally) Antipodes Islands. **Populations** Still recovering. Main rookeries on South Atlantic and South Indian Ocean islands. Does not yet breed in NZ territory, but may do so in future. **Status** Vagrant. **Management** None.

New Zealand sea lion *Phocarctos hookeri*

Family Otariidae. **Identification** Males dark brown, females creamy-grey to white, pups born dark brown, moult to silver-grey. Adult males with thick, coarse mane, otherwise coat sparse with no underfur; blunt snout, long whiskers. Dental formula I3/2, C1/1, PM4/4, M2/1 = 36. **Similar species** NZ fur seal much smaller,

Male.

with thicker fur, grey-brown in both sexes; subantarctic fur seal has yellow face and chest; all true seals lack external ears. **Size** Adult males average 320–450 kg, females 85–160 kg; pups 7–8 kg at birth. **NZ range** Southern South Island, Stewart, Auckland and Campbell Islands. In pre-human times, also ranged around all mainland coasts and to Chatham Islands. **Habitat** Flat sandy beaches, coastal dunes and forest up to 1 km from shore. Forage in shallow water over continental shelf. Average dive 3–4 minutes, to *c.* 120 m. **Food** Octopus, fish, occasional seabirds, penguins, and fur seal pups. **Social behaviour** Adult males haul out October–November, establish territories of *c.* 5 m diameter, defended by ritual posturing, charging, fierce fighting; only the largest few (*c.* 20%) territorial males get to breed. Females arrive December; aggregate in groups on beach until near parturition, then isolate themselves for birth. **Reproduction** Females produce first pup at 4 years; males mature at 5, but seldom hold territories till 8–10. Females produce pups alone, over short period mid December–mid January; establish immediate bond with it by smell and voice; suckle for *c.* 10 days, mate again with nearest territorial male, then return to sea for first short foraging trip. Pups >10 days old gather

Cow and pup.

in groups on beach while mothers away. Mothers return frequently to suckle mainly but not only own pup; after 4–6 weeks move pups to shelter inland, returning to suckle at gradually lengthening intervals; lead pups to sea in February; lactation continues *c.* 10 months. Can live to 25 years old. **Populations** Mainland populations hunted for meat by Maori. Fur less favoured by European sealers, but after 1815 accepted as substitute for rapidly disappearing NZ fur seals; all populations reduced to remnants by mid-1830s. Slowly increasing since all sealing ended in 1916, but still vulnerable to epidemic disease (e.g. 53% of pups on Auckland Islands died in January 1998, plus 20% in 2002) and drowning in trawl nets. Total population in 2000/01 *c.* 12,000. **Status** Endemic. **Management** IUCN status Threatened. Management of trawling bycatch (17–141/year in Auckland Islands squid fishery 1988–98) controlled by a theoretical model used to set maximum allowable bycatch, usually 60–80; when exceeded, MAF closes fishery early, inviting litigation contesting assumptions of the model from fishing interests.

True seals

TRUE SEALS

Family Phocidae: true seals

True seals have no external ears, and cannot turn their hind flippers forward, so they can move on land only by a series of inelegant humping motions like a caterpillar. Elephant seals and leopard seals are the only members of this group to visit the New Zealand mainland; the other three are all confined to the Antarctic. Males are much larger than females only in species that have stable breeding colonies and vigorous competition between males for mating rights.

Southern elephant seal *Mirounga leonina*

Family Phocidae. **Identification** Adults dark grey, pups born furred, black, silvery-grey by 3 weeks; adult hide with short, stiff hair, no underfur, massive blubber layer; males have large canines and inflatable proboscis on nose. During 4–6 weeks of catastrophic moult (females and juveniles November–January, males January–March), they lie in muddy wallows sloughing off hair and skin in large patches, at huge energy cost in enforced fasting and skin regrowth. When at sea, mean dive length 20 minutes, maximum 2 hours, to average of 400 m, often 1000 m. Dental formula I2/1,

Bull, cow and pup.

C1/1, Pm4/4, M1/1 = 30. **Similar species** Fur seals and sea lions have external ears; no other earless seal is so large and without any spots or streaks in fur. **Size** Males are the largest seals in the world, averaging 3500 kg, females 500 kg; pups 40 kg at birth. **NZ range** One of four main genetically independent breeding stocks spread around Antarctic has rookeries on Campbell and

Antipodes Islands. They visit Auckland, Snares, Stewart, Chatham and South Islands, and occasionally produce pups there. Some known individuals become regular visitors on mainland (e.g. 'Humphrey' on Coromandel/Bay of Plenty every summer for 5 years to 1989/90; 'Homer' over several years to 2000 at Christchurch, then Gisborne). **Habitat** Beaches, dunes and easily accessible flat coastal areas. 'Humphrey' used to visit a dairy farm and a caravan park, causing consternation (and some danger) to cows and campers. **Food** Squid, octopus, and fish, including deep-water species. **Social behaviour** Males haul out in August, but do not hold territories. They compete fiercely, mostly by posturing and roaring, or if necessary in fights, inflicting gruesome injuries on each other, until a dominance hierarchy is established. Dominant males, up to 10 times the weight of females, herd females into harems, and they achieve most matings, but females will also accept other males; many pups not sired by dominant male of local group. **Reproduction** Females haul out on land just before parturition in September; suckle pup on very rich milk for *c.* 3 weeks, mate in early November, then return to sea after total of 4 weeks' fasting ashore. Pups can triple their birth weight before mother leaves; then live 5–6 weeks on stored fat while learning to swim; leave for sea in December. Females mature at 4–7 years, then breed annually to 12–15 years old, some to 20; males mature at 5 years, but few under 12 can hold harems, and most do not survive that long. **Populations** Intensive harvesting for blubber oil ended in NZ region in 1830. Remaining NZ breeding population small (?<1000) and still declining, but South Atlantic population large (>450,000) and growing. **Status** Native. **Management** Protected.

Cow.

Leopard seal *Hydrurga leptonyx*

Female.

Family Phocidae. **Identification** Long, sinuous, well-furred body, blue-black above, sharply distinguished from silver below; large fore flippers (30% of total length), large flat-topped head with wide gape, few short whiskers. Long canines and complex, serrated molars. Dental formula I2/2, C1/1, Pm4/4, M1/1 = 32. **Similar species** Fur seals and sea lions have external ears; elephant seal very large, no spots; all other seals have smaller flippers, rounded heads. **Size** Both sexes average 275–500 kg; pups 30 kg at birth. **NZ range** Throughout Ross Dependency; occasionally visit southern

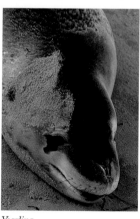

Yearling.

South Island. **Habitat** Pack ice and subantarctic islands, especially around penguin colonies. **Food** Krill, fish, penguins, fur seal pups. **Social behaviour** Communicate using at least 12 different underwater calls, some used during close-range hostile encounters, some broadcast by receptive females. The lowest frequency call is powerful enough to be audible at the surface and felt through the ice. **Reproduction** Females mature at 2–3 years, males at 4–6 years. Shifting pack ice prevents establishment of stable breeding groups monopolised by a dominant male; competition for mating rights minimal, so males are not much larger than females. Pups born on ice, October–November; mortality in first year about 25%; survivors can live 13–16 years. **Populations** Never exploited; current total population >200,000. **Status** Native. **Management** Protected.

Crabeater seal *Lobodon carcinophagus*

Family Phocidae. **Identification** Lithe, well-furred body, dark brown above, blond below, fading to entirely blond in summer (once called 'white Antarctic seal'); flippers dark. Small head with few, short whiskers; short canines, complex molars that fit perfectly together, forming an effective strainer. Dental formula I2/2, C1/1, Pm 4/4, M1/1 = 32. **Similar species** Fur seals and sea lions have external ears; elephant seal very large, no spots; Weddell seal has forward-projecting 'ice-cutter' front teeth; leopard seal has large head, white belly; Ross seal has thick neck, very large eyes. **Size** Both sexes average 200 kg; pups 30 kg at birth. **NZ range** Throughout Ross Dependency. **Habitat** Mainly on pack ice; occasionally found far inland on Antarctic continent. **Food** Mainly (*c.* 95% of diet) krill, sieved out of water through intricately lobed molars. Frequent (>200/day) short (3 minutes), shallow (10–40 m) dives into zone where krill most abundant, but also capable of much deeper (300–450 m) dives for at least 15 minutes at a time. One possible explanation is that these deep dives enable crabeater seals to escape surface noise (of ice floes grinding against each other in the swell) to listen for krill swarms. Krill move closer to surface at night, so crabeaters prefer to haul out by day and forage at night. **Social behaviour** Unsociable, living alone or in small groups of 2–3; female with pups often guarded by a male awaiting his turn. No vocal communication known. **Reproduction** Pups born on ice in October, suckle for only 17 days, gain weight at 4 kg/day; weaned in November at 80–110 kg. Females mate again before December; implantation delayed 81 days; active gestation 9 months. Both sexes mature at 6–7 years, most females pup every year. **Populations** Long-lived (>10% exceed 20 years, oldest known was 39) and never seriously exploited. Total population in the millions. **Status** Native. **Management** Protected.

Weddell seal *Leptonychotes weddellii*

Family Phocidae. **Identification** Body and most of flippers thickly furred, blue-black above, spotted with white on the belly, pups grey-brown; head small in proportion to large body, with short muzzle and whiskers, large deep brown eyes. Incisors and canines strong, projecting forward, used as cutters for keeping breathing holes open throughout winter in spaces between deep, perennial tide cracks in sea ice. Dental formula I2/2, C1/1, Pm4/4, M1/1 = 32. **Similar species** No other seal has a disproportionately small head with ice-cutter teeth. **Size** Both sexes vary between years, usually 350–500 kg; pups 24 kg at birth. **NZ range** Ross ice shelf, McMurdo Sound, Ross and White Islands, throughout Ross Sea. **Habitat** Permanent ice (up to 3 m thick, extending 400 km from coast in winter), ranging to edge of pack ice. **Food** Mainly fish and squid, from throughout water column and sea floor under ice; occasionally also penguins. Adults dive on average to 150 m for 10 minutes per trip. **Social behaviour** Strongly vocal, producing 21–44 recognisably distinct, complex calls. Males establish underwater territories near deep cracks in permanent sea ice, defended by almost continuous calling. Females form breeding groups in same areas. Breathing holes shared. **Reproduction** Males fertile October–December; pups born on ice surface in October. Females stay with pups for first 12 days, then nearby until end of lactation (6 weeks), losing more than half their body weight while pup increases from 25 to 110 kg. Females mate in the water in December; delay in implantation short (1–2 months); produce first pup at 2–6 years old, then annually to age *c.* 18. Males mature at 3 years, but do not attend breeding colonies until 5–7, generally unsuccessfully until age 8–13. Pups start diving after 2 weeks; by 6 weeks can dive to 50–70 m for 3–4 minutes; by 12 weeks, to 100 m for 5–6 minutes. **Populations** Annual survival rate of adults *c.* 85%, much less (30–60%) in pups and young (ages 0–6). Formerly (until 1986) killed to support expeditions and for dog meat, but dogs now banned from Antarctica, and humans bring own supplies. Tourist ships can enter Ross Sea only after January, after seals finish breeding. Population in McMurdo Sound *c.* 2500–3000; in world, *c.* 1 million. **Status** Native. **Management** Protected.

Ross seal *Ommatophoca rossi*

Family Phocidae. **Identification** Small, graceful body, dark brown above, silvery below with spots, streaks; very short body hairs; broad head, thick neck, short snout, few whiskers; large eyes (generic name means 'eye-seal'). Fore flippers with small claws and very long toes. Teeth small. Dental formula I2/2 C1/1 Pm4/4, M1/1 = 32. **Similar species** Fur seals and sea lions have external ears; all other earless seals larger than Ross. **Size** Both sexes average 130–200 kg; pups 20 kg at birth. **NZ range** Ross Sea. **Habitat** Seldom seen on pack ice except when breeding or moulting; at other times of year they spend long periods in open water of Ross Sea. **Food** Squid, octopus, fish, some krill. One tagged individual averaged 113 dives/day, to all depths from 12 to 400 m. **Social behaviour** Apparently unsociable (most seen alone, <10% seen in pairs), although lone seals often associates with several others under ice, communicating with each other with loud calls, amplified by resonating chambers in larynx and large soft palate. **Reproduction** Pups born November, females mate December, implantation delayed till March. Females mature at age 2–4 years, males at 3–4, both may live *c.* 20 years. **Populations** Never exploited, but vulnerable to killer whales when at sea far from ice. Total probably >100,000. **Status** Native. **Management** Protected.

© SeaPics.com

Mustelids: stoats, weasels and ferrets

Family Mustelidae

European rabbits reached plague numbers in 1870s New Zealand, driving sheep farmers to ruin in ways unknown back 'Home'. Foxes were unwelcome, so the colonial government sent out an official request for mustelids, reputed to be great rabbiters but no threat to lambs. With official sanction, three species of passage-paid experts in rabbit destruction were imported and released all round the country by government agents and farmers, ignoring protests from ornithologists. This massive, uncontrolled experiment in biological control was ultimately fruitless, since rabbits control numbers of their predators, not vice versa. It was also tragic, because, unlike rats, cats, dogs and human hunters, mustelids could have been prevented from reaching New Zealand; by 1900 they were adding to the already inevitable destruction of native fauna.

All mustelids have long bodies and short legs; black eyes with vivid green eyeshine; large scent gland under tail, capable of producing a 'stink bomb' when threatened. Males are much larger than females, and have an *os baculum* (penile bone), conspicuously larger in adults than young.

Stoat *Mustela erminea*

Male.

Family Mustelidae. **Identification** Summer coat brown above, white below; long thin tail brown with bushy black tip, fluffed into 'bottlebrush' when excited. In colder areas (southern South Island and/or higher elevations), may turn partly or entirely white except for black tail tip. Confidently climbs trees to great heights and swims 1–2 km. Dental formula I3/3, C1/1, Pm3/3, M1/2 = 34. **Similar species** Weasel smaller, with no black tip to the tail; ferret larger, with no distinct white belly and face often with dark mask across eyes. **Size** Adult males average 325 g, head–body length 280 mm, tail 100 mm; females 200 g, 260 mm, 90 mm. **NZ range** Rapid

Male with seagull egg.

spread after first introductions in 1884 throughout North and South Islands; from sea level to limit of vegetation; swam to *c.* 37 inshore islands; never taken to or reached many other valuable conservation islands further than 2 km offshore (e.g. Stewart or Chatham). Eradicated from Maud (twice), Anchor, Chalky Islands; operations in progress on other important islands including Secretary, Resolution. **Habitat** Earliest releases all on rabbit-infested pastures, but quickly moved to and through areas with no rabbits. Now the most common carnivore in forests, but much less common than ferrets in open country, except in gullies, scrub and long grass with many mice. **Food** Birds, eggs, mice, rabbits, rats, possums, lizards, and insects, especially weta, varying with habitat. Killing behaviour stimulated by alarm reaction of prey, independent of hunger; surplus prey cached for future use. Climbs trees to raid nests, and follows rabbits and kiwi into burrows, but cannot prevent irruptions of rats or mice after a heavy seedfall. **Social behaviour** Solitary, active any time. Social communication via individually distinct scent signals. **Reproduction** Breeding season closely synchronised by day length. Males mature at 10 months, females as unweaned nestlings 3–5 weeks old. Adult females and all their female young mated in November, but implantation delayed until following August; active gestation 4 weeks; kits born in September/October. Litter size averages 8–10 at conception, maximum 18, reduced by intrauterine/nestling mortality in proportion to food supplies during birth season 10 months later, if necessary to zero. Young blind, naked, 3–4 g at birth; eyes open at 5–6 weeks, fully furred at 8 weeks; weaned at 7–12 weeks. Young born when food abundant grow slightly larger than normal, but young born in other years live longer. **Populations** Proportion of young trapped depends mainly on success of previous breeding season, so populations dynamic and variable between years. Few live to 3 years old. **Status** Introduced. **Management** Major pest. Vulnerable native birds including bush wrens, NZ thrush, saddleback, laughing owl, South Island kokako, kakapo, takahe and kiwi, still abundant in Fiordland/Westland when stoats and ship rats first arrived in mid-1880s, but then suddenly disappeared. Now, *during* (not, as usually assumed, after) periodic irruptions of mice following heavy beech seedfalls, unusual numbers of stoats still cause great damage to native birds (mohua, kaka, parakeets, bellbirds) in South Island beech forests, and consequent low fruit set of native mistletoe. In North Island, huge mortality of unprotected chicks of kiwi and shorebirds attributed largely to stoats (and dogs). However, rats and cats arrived 100 years earlier than stoats, and rats are much more widely distributed. Stoats never contacted 112 of 167 separate populations of native birds lost since human settlement; are now much less abundant than ship rats; and are probably secondary to rats as threats to most surviving mainland species. Removal of stoats alone does not help threatened fauna if that permits rats to increase; effective management of all predators needed, by multispecies programmes or exclusion fencing.

Male with kaka killed on nest.

Weasel *Mustela nivalis*

Family Mustelidae. **Identification** Summer coat brown above, white below, brown spot under chin at corners of mouth; short brown tail with no black tip; never turns white in NZ; otherwise very similar to stoat except in reproductive cycle. Dental formula I3/3, C1/1, Pm3/3; M1/2 = 34. **Similar species** Stoat larger, always with bushy black tip to tail; ferret much larger, with no distinct white belly and face often with dark mask across eyes. **Size** Males average 220 g, females 180 g; head–body 125 mm, 60 mm; tail 50 mm, 40 mm. **NZ range** Introduced for same reasons as stoat, at same time and in greater numbers; spread similarly, but now much less common. **Habitat** Prefers thick ground cover teeming with mice – a habitat only intermittently available in NZ. May turn up unpredictably almost anywhere, especially where stoats are rare. **Food** Specialist predator of voles and lemmings (mouse-like rodents, absent in NZ). Mice, lizards, weta, birds, eggs are nearest but insufficient local substitutes. Rarely tackles rabbits except as kits or carrion. **Social behaviour** Solitary, active any time. **Reproduction** When food abundant, both sexes can mature in season of own birth and adults can produce a second, summer litter, but this is probably rare in NZ. Mating season September; gestation 35–37 days with no delayed implantation; litter size 4–6. Kits born blind, naked, in October at 1–2 g, furred by 3 weeks, eyes open 4 weeks; can kill mice at 8 weeks; independent by 9–12 weeks. **Populations** Numbers vary between years and places, ranging from unexpected abundance to local extinction, never stable. Very few live to as much as 1 year old. **Status** Introduced. **Management** Pest. Much less likely than stoats to reach protected birds on offshore islands; on mainland, damage overlaps with that of stoats.

Female.

Ferret *Mustela furo*

Female with newborn young.

Family Mustelidae. **Identification** Body with creamy-white underfur, long black guard hairs; back not brown; face often with dark mask across eyes; tail black, thick, bushy; legs black. Domesticated ferrets bred into a great variety of artificial fur colours; feral ferrets variable but most revert to wild type colour. When trapped, much less aggressive than stoats, which were never domesticated. Poor climbers and reluctant swimmers. Dental formula I3/3, C1/1, Pm3/3, M1/2 = 34. **Similar species** Stoat and weasel both smaller, brown above, white below, but stoat always has bushy black tip to tail; weasel has shorter tail with no black tip. **Size** Males average 1200 g, females 600 g; head–body 400 mm, 350 mm; tail 160 mm, 130 mm. **NZ range** First few imported from Australian rabbiters in late 1860s, then from UK in thousands over 20 years from 1882, and bred locally until 1912, all for wide release on rabbit-infested pastures. Second wave of importations in 1980s from Scottish and Finnish breeders of fancy-coloured strains for fur farms; escapes (or, when fur farming collapsed, releases) helped spread ferrets to new areas, e.g. Northland, Westland. Absent from Stewart and all offshore islands. **Habitat** Found wherever there are rabbits and cover, e.g. among scrub and briar patches on valley flats and tussock grasslands, along streams and overgrown gullies through improved pastures. Present but less common in bush margins, road verges and swamps. **Food** Primarily mammals (especially rabbits, possums, rats); also lizards, frogs, eels, invertebrates, ground-nesting birds and their eggs, and carrion including possums and other ferrets dead from TB. Can follow rabbits through underground burrows in total darkness, lying up there when satiated, and cache surplus kills. **Social behaviour** Unsociable, nocturnal. Social communication by complex, informative scent marking. **Reproduction** Breeding season August–September; gestation 41–42 days with no delay in implantation; litter size 4–8, up to 12; kits born blind, with fine white natal hair; eyes open at 30 days, fully furred in adult colours by 50 days; weaned at 6–8 weeks; 30–50% die before independence. Well-fed females can produce a second litter in late summer, but rarely do so successfully. Juveniles disperse at 3 months, on average 5–6 km, up to 45 km. **Populations** NZ has largest known population of truly feral ferrets. Numbers can reach up to 8/sq km; long-term average on semi-arid pastoral farmland of South Island 2–3/sq km, much less in North Island. Numbers seen dead on road vary with season, elevation and rabbit abundance. Recruitment and survival of young highest after resident adults culled; most live 1–3 years after independence. **Status** Introduced. **Management** Pest. Scavenging habits plus long-distance dispersal make ferrets important agents in spreading bovine TB, though it would not persist in them if eradicated from possums. Fer-

Scandinavian ferret bred for pelt.

rets kill adult kiwi, penguins, shorebirds, black stilt, weka, and destroy many nests. Control operations aim to prevent ferrets spreading TB, and minimise losses to ground-nesting birds.

Male feeding on penguin carcase.

Cats

Family Felidae

Domestic cats were commonly carried on sailing ships to control rats and mice, so were inevitably among the first European mammals to reach many New Zealand islands. Also carried on wagons inland with traders and settlers, but fully independent feral populations were rare for the first 50 years, perhaps in part because Maori valued them, like kuri, for meat and skins.

CATS

Feral cat *Felis catus*

Family Felidae. **Identification** Similar in appearance and variety of coat colours to domestic moggies, but much shyer and more aggressive when cornered. Dental formula I3/3, C1/1, Pm3/2, M1/1 = 30. **Similar species** Possum-like at a distance, but possum moves more awkwardly on ground. Possum tail naked at the end; toes form grasping hands not padded paws; claws not retractable. **Size** Males 2–4 kg, females 2–3 kg; head–body 500–550 mm. **NZ range** Spread widely by sealers, lighthouse keepers, settlers and farmers throughout mainland and 31 other islands to control rabbits and rodents; now eradicated or died out from at least 14 islands including key conservation sites (Little Barrier, Tiritiri Matangi, Cuvier, Kapiti, Stephens, Mangere); still present on Stewart, Chatham, Auckland, Great Barrier Islands. **Habitat** Forest of all sorts, scrub, grassland and farms, at all elevations. **Food** Primarily mammals (rabbits, rats, possums, mice), plus birds, lizards, invertebrates and carrion. Hunting by cats can have substantial effect on rabbit numbers, especially in small confined areas. On islands with no rabbits or rodents, cats take many more birds, mainly seabirds but also land birds already rare or extinct on mainland. **Social behaviour** Semi-sociable or solitary, active day or night, depending on circumstances. **Reproduction** Gestation 65 days, litters

Female feeding on a penguin it has killed.

2–5 kits born October–December; well-fed adults can produce a second litter in autumn. Kits remain in natal den for 5–6 weeks (to 500 g), then moved by mother to series of temporary dens. Adults can live 6–9 years, but juvenile survival poor where rabbits or rats scarce. **Populations** On good farmland, 3–5 cats/sq km possible; elsewhere, up to 3–5 sq km per cat. **Status** Introduced. **Management** Major pest. Historic damage by cats to native fauna hard to separate from that of European rats and mustelids on mainland, but cats still contribute to losses of kiwi, dotterels, black stilt, and lizards. Local or total extinctions can be attributed to cats on islands not reached by other predators, e.g. Stephens Island (wrens, saddlebacks, kokako) and Herekopare (parakeets, robins, snipe, rails, petrels); cats also contributed, with kiore, to losses on Cuvier (saddlebacks) and Little Barrier (saddlebacks, snipe), and with Norway rats until 2002, to devastation of birds on Raoul Island. Some of these species have already been returned from other islands since cats eradicated; planned restoration of Raoul will be possible when cats gone, because most species lost from Raoul still abundant on adjacent Meyer Island. Urban house cats kill many birds, but night curfews protect rodents, not birds; dumping of unwanted cats in rural areas is cruel and irresponsible.

Female.

Horses

Order Perissodactyla, Family Equidae

The odd-toed ungulates (perissodactyls) are a small group today (16 species of horses, donkeys, zebras, tapirs and rhinos). But between 54 and 25 million years ago, the perissodactyls were the dominant large mammals throughout the world, including many species now extinct. The perissodactyls have a simple and not very effective digestive system, which is perhaps why they are now less widespread in the wild than the even-toed ruminants (almost 200 species of cattle, deer, antelopes and goats). Nevertheless, members of one family of perissodactyls, the equids, have survived and prospered as domestic animals, and exerted an incalculable influence on human history.

Feral horse *Equus caballus*

Family Equidae. **Identification**. Mostly bay or chestnut, often with black mane, tail, legs; some black, roan or grey. Still very similar to domestic horses except that ferals are more shy; stallions have powerful necks, and are aggressive when cornered. No true wild horses ever brought to NZ; 'wild' horses here are merely feral domestics. Dental formula I3/3, C1/1, Pm3–4/3, M3/3 = 42. **Similar species** None. **Size** In conventional horse measurements, most are 14–15 hands tall at the shoulders (*c.* 1.5 m). Derived from escaped British cavalry mounts crossed with local domestic stock largely from Exmoor/Welsh pony stock. **NZ range** Imported with European settlers from 1814, and mounted regiments from 1840 onwards. Escapes and strays gathered in semi-feral herds, once common in the North Island and Chathams; culling has limited them to two

Two mares with immatures.

distinct herds, in NZ Army training area in Kaimanawa Mountains near Waiouru, and in Aupouri Forest, Northland. **Habitat** Prefer a mosaic of grassland for grazing and shrubs or light forest for shelter. **Food** Native and introduced grasses, tussocks, sedges and herbs. Simple (non-ruminant) digestion. Horse grazing causes measurable changes in vegetation, including to rare plants of high local significance. **Social behaviour** Social, diurnal. Herds comprise a group of mares and their foals led by a dominant stallion (if several stallions, one clearly ranks higher than the others). Other males live alone or in a loose bachelor group. Social rank determined by threat behaviour, ranging from flattened ears to rearing and striking out with forelegs. **Reproduction** Age at maturity 3–4 years; females fertile in spring, males all year. Gestation 11 months; foals born with woolly natal coat, eyes open, in October–December; can stand and suckle within 2 hours, follow mother within 5 hours; lactation lasts *c.* 6–10 months. Younger mares breed only every second year, and are less successful in raising foals to independence. **Populations** Kaimanawa herd *c.* 500; Aupouri herd *c.* 300. **Status** Introduced. **Management** Pest. Kaimanawa herd maintained, at level agreed between DoC and public, by periodic mustering and sale of surplus young into private ownership; Aupouri herd unmanaged.

Cloven-hoofed ungulates

Order Artiodactyla: pigs, cattle, goats and goat allies, deer

More cloven-hoofed ungulates were brought to New Zealand than any other type of mammal, because they were perceived to be useful as farm stock or as sporting targets. Many farm animals escaped and established independent feral populations, but they are still different from their true wild (pre-domesticated) ancestors.

Pigs

Family Suidae: pigs

Pigs were common in the Polynesian islands 1000 years ago, but none was brought on, or none survived, the voyage to New Zealand with the ancestors of the Maori. Most 'wild' pigs in New Zealand are feral descendants of European domestic breeds that have reverted to boar-like appearance. There are also some feral groups of kune kune, a domestic breed of Asian origin.

Feral pig *Sus scrofa*

Family Suidae. **Identification** Stocky, muscular bodies with long legs, massive shoulders and narrow hindquarters; eyes small and sight poor, but sense of smell and hearing acute. Narrow back (so, also called 'razorbacks'); tail straight with brushy tip; long snout with large tusks, and short ears; hair long, coarse, varying in colour with founder breed, mostly black but also reddish-ginger, brown and white, grey to blue-grey, some with spots or a dark dorsal stripe. Piglets may be striped. Dental formula I3/3, C1/1, Pm4/4, M3/3 = 44. **Similar species** Domestic pig broader in the back, much less hairy, shorter snout, longer ears, tail often curly. European wild boar is similar in appearance to NZ feral pig, but was never brought to NZ. Kune kune is smaller, fatter, and has a distinctive pair of fleshy tassels hanging from the lower jaw. **Size** Adult males 45–200 kg; height at shoulder 550–950 mm; tail 200–450 mm; females 30–115 kg, 450–600 mm, 200–450 mm. **NZ range** Maori greatly valued pigs from first contact, so early Europeans from James Cook onwards used pigs as gifts and in trade, and released them on islands as food for shipwreck survivors. Once established, feral populations rapidly spread unaided. Now occupy *c.* 100,000 sq km, plus 13 islands including Chatham and Auckland Islands, but have died out or been eradicated from 27 other islands. Official control operations 1950–85 reduced their range, but withdrawal of subsidised control and greater interest by hunters helped to reverse that effect in the 1990s. **Habitat** Native and exotic forest, marginal or reverting farmland, river flats and scrub, provided there is accessible water and cover. Frosts that restrict digging keep pigs out of high country in winter. **Food** Digestion is simple (non-ruminant) and rather inefficient; can survive on low-quality fibrous food but cannot breed (and young cannot grow) without adequate protein. Pigs eat fruits, fungi, bracken, possum carrion; use snouts to dig for roots, tubers, snails, worms; may take weak lambs and cast sheep; on islands, search beaches for seaweed and cast-up fish and seabirds. **Social behaviour** Females and young sociable, adult males generally solitary; active any time. **Reproduction** Can breed at 25 kg (5–8 months), much earlier than in Australia. Main mating season April–June, but possible throughout the year. Gestation 112–114 days, most litters born July–November; 2 litters a year common, or 3 in 16 months. Litter size 6; each piglet takes possession of a particular teat, suckles in natal nest for 2–3 weeks, then follows mother out foraging; weaned at 6–10 weeks. **Populations** By mid-19th century, feral pigs were abundant (annual kills in thousands for decades), but declined as food became scarce. National population now >100,000, sustaining harvests of from <10 to >20 pigs/sq km. Most pigs live only 1 year or less, varying with food supplies and harvesting intensity. **Status** Introduced. **Management** Mixed. Earliest irruptions of pig numbers through untouched forests massively destructive to ground-nesting birds, snails and invertebrates, but damage now indistinguishable from those of rats and cats. On Auckland Islands pigs severely damage endemic megaherbs and seabird nests. Conversely, hunters regard pigs as a valuable resource.

Boar (top); sow with piglets (above).

Cattle, goats and goat allies

Family Bovidae: cattle, chamois, tahr, goat, sheep

All bovids are medium to large mammals with permanent horns in both sexes. They have a multi-chambered stomach and a two-stage (ruminant) digestive system. First, they spend the minimum possible time with their heads down in the open collecting food in mouthfuls and swallowing it whole. Then they retreat to safe cover, regurgitate the food one lump at a time, and grind it up finely ('chewing the cud') with their heads up watching out for predators. Only after the second trip past the teeth does each mouthful go on to the digestion chambers. This system is very efficient, and bovids are a large and successful family. Five different bovids have been brought to New Zealand: three as domestic stock (cattle, sheep and goats), and two for sport (chamois, Himalayan tahr).

Feral cattle *Bos taurus*

Cow.

Family Bovidae. **Identification** Most derived from European breeds, quite different from ancestral stock or genuine wild cattle of other countries. Large body, long tufted tail, horns spreading sideways, short coat, no beard, mane or scent glands. Males much larger than females. Distinguishable from domestic stock only by their lack of ear tags. Dental formula I0/3, C0/1, Pm3/3, M3/3 = 32. **Similar species** None. **Size** Much as domestic cattle; some have proportionately higher shoulders and narrower hindquarters than modern farm animals, especially mature males. **NZ range** Brought with earliest European settlers and traders, from 1814 onwards. Fencing on pioneer farms was often lacking or insecure, so cattle soon lost or escaped mustering, and ran wild. Mobs of

100+ reported on main islands in 1860s–80s, and were hunted for sport; numbers gradually diminished, and by 1980s reduced to 15 distinct herds. Many of those on mainland back country, plus Stewart, Enderby and Campbell Islands, have now been exterminated because of their potential to harbour bovine TB, or their damage to conservation values. **Habitat** Prefer thick scrub for cover, on easy slopes within range of clearings with tussock grasses; on Campbell Island, lived only on a small area underlain by limestone. In bush they can lay bare the forest floor and prevent all regeneration of palatable species. **Food** Grass, ferns and browse from a great variety of shrubs and low trees. **Social behaviour** Sociable, active by day, much shyer and more alert than farm animals. Females and young form family groups with a mature bull; other males live in bachelor groups or alone. In breeding season males roar, smash shrubs and paw the ground. **Reproduction** Males mature at 1 year but cannot compete for females until much older. Females produce first calf at 3 years, and live for about 12 years. Gestation 9.5 months; calves born with eyes open, stand and suckle at once, follow mother within hours. **Populations** Most groups small; calving rates often poor, depending on food supply (e.g. 10–25% on Campbell, 47–67% on Enderby). **Status** Introduced. **Management** Pest, also possibly a historic resource. The Enderby population has been isolated from other cattle since 1896, so could represent a 'primitive' breed. One cow ('Lady') survived the 1990 extermination, was rescued and returned to NZ mainland; attempts are being made to reconstitute the breed (total herd reached 7 in 2002).

Chamois *Rupicapra rupicapra*

Family Bovidae. **Identification** Slender body similar to goat but with longer legs and neck, and larger hooves; summer coat light brown with dark face stripe and white chin, winter coat thicker, dark brown to black, with prominent mane in males; short tail, small black horns erect and hooked, short coat, no beard, scent glands behind horns and in front of eyes. Large eyes and excellent sight. Athletic, graceful animals with astonishing agility in steep terrain. Males and females much the same size. Dental formula I0/3, C0/1, Pm3/3, M3/3 = 32. **Similar species** No other ungulate has upright hooked horns in both sexes. **Size** Smaller than in Europe. Males eviscerated weight 16–20 kg, body length 1.1–1.2 m; females 14–20 kg, 1.1–1.2 m; kids 2.5–3.5 kg at birth. **NZ range** Ten chamois arrived in NZ from Austria in 1907 and 1914 as a gift to NZ Government from Emperor Franz Josef II; released near Mt Cook; rapidly spread throughout Southern Alps, still reaching new areas despite efforts to contain them. Present range *c.* 50,000 sq km. **Habitat** Steep alpine/subalpine grassland and rocky bluffs above tree line, extending into high elevation forest in Westland. **Food** Tussock grasses, herbs and alpine woody plants. **Social behaviour** Semi-sociable, diurnal. Chamois form loose matriarchal groups dispersed over 2–7 sq km; within group, females and young stay together, males mostly solitary. Individual home ranges marked with scent; intolerance between females keeps group well spread out; aggression between males confined mainly to posturing and chasing. **Reproduction** Mature at 1.5–2.5 years old, rut May–July, gestation 170 days; single kid born November–December. When food abundant, yearling females can also produce a kid, but later in season (February). Kids can follow mother within an hour; grow rapidly (to 15 kg by 7 months when food abundant); full grown at age 3 years. **Populations** Local groups comprise dynamic core of resident adults plus non-resident migrants quick to replace any

Kid.

lost members of core group. Life expectancy at birth 3–4 years, maximum 15–20 years. Survival and productivity in relatively mild climate of NZ is good by European standards, despite epidemics of facial eczema and competition with tahr. Total numbers *c.* 20,000. **Status** Introduced. **Management** Mixed. Browsing damage cannot be distinguished from that of tahr, goats, deer, but *c.* 90,000 chamois shot in control programmes 1930s–1982. Not endangered in native range. Valued for game trophies/meat.

Female in summer coat.

Gordon Roberts

Female (with horns) with two young in winter.

Gordon Roberts

95

Himalayan tahr *Hemitragus jemlahicus*

Family Bovidae. **Identification** Robust body, dark to grey brown with dense underhair shed in spring; males with long shaggy straw-coloured mane; short tail bare underneath; short stout horns curving backwards, no beard, no scent glands. Excellent eyesight. Hooves with soft pad in centre, and patches of short dense hair on chest and backs of legs. Males much larger than females. Dental formula I0/3, C0/1, Pm 3/3, M3/3 = 32. **Similar species** Chamois has slender, black, upright horns; goat has longer horns, either in an erect scimitar form or spreading sideways in an open spiral, males with a beard; deer have deciduous antlers not permanent horns, in males only. **Size** Adult males 70 kg, carcase 50 kg, body length 1.6 m, horns 300 mm; females 35 kg, 25 kg, 1.3 m, 180 mm. Kids *c.* 2 kg at birth. **NZ range** Introduced by NZ Government to provide hunting for residents and tourists; 13 released near Mt Cook in 1904, 1909, multiplied to 50 by 1918; the three released near Rotorua in 1909 did not establish a population. At peak of expansion, South Island breeding populations occupied >6000 sq km centred on Mt Cook; now reduced to *c.* 4300 sq km. Recent range expansions due to illegal releases. **Habitat** Rock bluffs, alpine grassland, subalpine shrubland and upper forest. Typically rest through middle of day at high elevation, descending to feed in afternoon, returning next day. **Food** Snow tussocks, alpine herbs and shrubs. **Social behaviour** Sociable, diurnal. Large social groups with no strong hierarchy, segregated by age and sex until the rut; then mixed until early summer, when males leave female range. After parturition in December, previous year's kids gather in separate, transient yearling groups near adult females. **Reproduction** Males attain full breeding coat at 4.5 years; compete for

Gordon Roberts

Bull.

females by ritualised posturing with mane erect, 'parallel walking' or chasing, fights rare. Rut May–July; age at first breeding in females depends on food supplies and local numbers. Gestation 165 days; single kid born November–January; can nurse within half an hour, and walk unsteadily within a day, but usually left hidden while mother grazes nearby for a few days before rejoining female group. **Populations** Peak numbers *c.* 30–40,000 in 1970 (to 30/sq km in places) reduced by commercial game-meat hunting and aerial control to <2000 in 1984, now at least 9000 (1–2/sq km). **Status** Introduced. **Management** Mixed. At high densities tahr damage to snow tussocks can be locally severe, e.g. during 1960s–70s. But tahr are also highly valued for game trophies/meat; there is strong demand for adult males by NZ and overseas hunters. Total eradication strongly opposed by hunters, and impossible in any case. Moratorium on all hunting 1983–94 allowed public consultation; result is an official management plan granting primary control over most of the range to recreational hunters, provided they keep tahr numbers below locally damaging levels (2.5 tahr/sq km); failing that, and in national parks and at the northern and southern range boundaries, official control operations triggered.

Nanny and kid.

Gordon Roberts

Feral goat *Capra hircus*

Family Bovidae. **Identification** Slim muscular body, varied in coat (short or long), texture (rough or silky), colour (brown/black/white), ears (erect or floppy), throat lappets (present or absent), all reflecting founder breeds; short tufted tail bare underneath, may be carried erect, beard on males and some females, short mane on males. Horns either spreading sideways or swept back in a spiral. Scent glands on front feet and under tail. Prominent yellow eyes, good sight and hearing. Males slightly larger than females. Dental formula I0/3, C0/1, Pm3/3, M3/3 = 32. **Similar species** Chamois has slender, black, upright horns; Himalayan tahr has short horns curving sharply back, males with a prominent mane;

Male.

deer have deciduous antlers not permanent horns, in males only. **Size** Adult males 40 kg, carcase 22 kg, body length 1.3 m, height at the shoulder 70 cm; females 30 kg, 15 kg, 1.1 m, 60 cm. Kids 2 kg at birth. **NZ range** Goats were often carried on sailing ships for fresh meat, and provided hardy stock for pioneer farms, weed control and castaway islands. First goats landed by James Cook in 1773 and 1777; from then onwards throughout 19th century, goats liberated widely on mainland NZ and to at least 34 islands, including some of great conservation value (Auckland, Antipodes, Campbell, Cuvier, Kapiti, Maud, Raoul, Macauley). Later introductions of specialist dairy or fibre breeds also added their genes to the mainland feral population, which now occupies *c.* 40,000 sq km of both main islands and four offshore islands (Arapawa, Forsyth, Great Barrier, Great Mercury). **Habitat** Forest, scrub and grassland of all sorts, especially on steep ground inaccessible to the less agile deer or sheep. **Food** Primarily browsers, with wide tastes but also some strong preferences, especially certain native shrubs such as broadleaf and mahoe. Can change the composition of forest vegetation; expose forest floor; inhibit regeneration on steep, eroding slopes; climb sloping tree trunks to reach favoured flowers; and, if held in high numbers, can combat invasions by blackberry and sweet briar. **Social behaviour** Compulsively sociable, diurnal. Females and kids live in rather sedentary matriarchal groups, collected into loose aggregations; young and mature males in separate groups, except during the rut; all playful even as adults. **Reproduction** Dominant males >4 years old mate often, others less often or not at all. Feral goats retain the characters, bred into them by Neolithic farmers, which make them much more serious pests than their true wild ancestors, including non-seasonal breeding (kids born any time), early maturity (females can breed at 6 months) and high productivity (twins common, increasing with age; average 1.1–1.4 kids/female/year). Gestation 150 days; newborn kid kept hidden for *c.* 4 days, then mother-kid pair gradually rejoin group. **Populations** Numbers can range from <1–10/ha, depending on food supplies and harvesting pressure. On Raoul Island over a 10-year eradication programme, reduced numbers stimulated massive demographic compensation, which decreased population-doubling time to 20 months. **Status** Introduced. **Management** Major pest but with minor value for weed control and to Rare Breeds Conservation Society. Goats can be eradicated in forested areas by teams of experienced hunters with well-trained dogs, provided there are no refuges, no immigrants, and goats can be removed faster than they can be replaced. Radio-collared 'Judas' goats can lead hunters to any survivors. Arapawa Island goats supposed by some to represent last surviving Old English breed.

Feral sheep *Ovis aries*

Ram.

Family Bovidae. **Identification** Chunky body, long woolly tail, long crimped white or dark brown to black fleece. No beard or mane, scent glands on all feet. Proportion with horns, spiralling back in tight curls, or scurs (horny pads not visible above fleece) varies locally. Males slightly larger than females. Dental formula I0/3, C0/1, Pm3/3, M3/3 = 32. **Similar species** No other ungulate has crimped fleece. **Size** Adults 40–50 kg; body length 1.2 m, shoulder height 70 cm. **NZ range** Domestic sheep of various breeds have been imported and widely distributed throughout 19th and 20th centuries, including to at least 10 outlying islands to stock farms or support castaways. Sheep lost from unfenced ranges, or abandoned

Ram.

on failed farms, gathered into feral flocks that were once common in remote areas of both main islands. Eradications have reduced these to seven separate groups on mainland and four on islands. **Habitat** Rough pasture with broken scrub for shelter. **Food** Primarily graze on grass and herbs, occasionally browse scrub. On Campbell Island sheep and fire almost eliminated the endemic megaherbs. **Social behaviour** Sociable, diurnal. Ewe with young of year the most stable social group; rams form separate group outside rut. **Reproduction** Mating mainly June–July, gestation 150 days, lambing rate *c*. 20–80%, growth slower than in farm stock. **Populations** First five sheep arriving in 1814 were Australian merinos, replaced by 1900 (except in South Island high country) with cross-bred European breeds. Most fleeces are or were white on mainland, Campbell and Chatham Islands; most dark and self-shedding on Arapawa and Pitt. On Campbell Island (11,200 ha), sheep farmed 1895–1931, then abandoned. Numbers declined from 8500 in 1916 to <1000 in 1961, then recovered after three Cheviot rams were introduced in 1953 to improve the stock. **Status** Introduced. **Management** Pest. The potential for spectacular recovery of native vegetation was demonstrated when Campbell Island was bisected by a fence in 1970, and 1300 feral sheep shot on the northern side. In 1984 another 4000 were removed from the southern side, and in 1989–90 the last 1400 from Mt Paris peninsula. Numbers on other islands are or were much smaller. All NZ feral sheep are derived from modern breeds, of minor historical interest.

Ram and lamb.

Deer

Family Cervidae

Deer-stalking was the sport of the aristocracy in 19th-century Europe, but settlers in New Zealand seized the chance to stock huge areas of apparently empty public land with fine game animals available to lesser folk. Eleven species of deer (one with two distinct subspecies) were imported from Europe, America and Asia; all but three established wild populations, some in numbers exceeding all expectations.

Like bovids, deer are alert, fast-running, cloven-hoofed ruminants. The main difference is that deer have antlers, made of naked bone (no horny sheath), grown and shed every year by males only, in contrast to the permanent horns worn by both sexes of bovids.

Red deer *Cervus elaphus scoticus*

Family Cervidae. **Identification** Antlers round, erect, 10+ tines; coat plain red-brown in summer, grey-brown in winter; rump patch medium size, creamy-white, bordered with long black stripe; tail short, red-brown; black hairless muzzle; calves spotted until *c.* 2 months old. Dental formula I0/3, C1/1, Pm3/3, M3/3 = 34. **Similar species** Wapiti has plain brown adult coat, large creamy rump patch extending onto lower back, short white tail; sika has spotted adult coat in summer, plain in winter, long white tail with black stripe; sambar has plain brown adult coat, large rounded ears, small creamy-white rump patch, long brown tail; rusa has plain brown adult coat, small light brown rump patch, long brown tail; fallow

Roaring stag.

Calf.

has spotted or plain coat in several shades of brown to black, white or brown rump patch, long black and/or white tail; white-tailed deer has plain brown adult coat, white rump patch, long brown tail with white fringe. **Size** Adult males 100 kg, carcase 70 kg, length 1.8 m; females 75 kg, 50 kg, 1.7 m. **NZ range** Multiple introductions recorded throughout North (except Northland, Waikato and Taranaki), South and Stewart Islands (original stock *c.* 250 animals from UK plus their descendants, total *c.* 1000 by 1923), all of mixed farm/park parentage. Released in groups of 6–10 at >50 known release sites. Rapid natural spread; now can be found in suitable places over 120,000 sq km of mainland (most often in about half that area of tall forest offering shelter from aerial hunting; least often in areas easily accessible to recreational hunters). Swims well; occupies or visits many inshore islands including Secretary and Resolution. Still spreading into new areas, sometimes with (illegal) human help. **Habitat** Native and exotic forests of all sorts, from sea level to limit of vegetation; river flats, grassland and swamps. Sustained hunting often excludes them from alpine grasslands above timber line and, unless protected by landowner, from farm margins and crops. **Food** Farmed deer can live entirely on pasture; wild deer mix browsing with grazing according to opportunity. Red deer eat 1–3 kg dry matter per day on farms, <1 kg in the wild; browse leaves and bark of preferred species (fuchsia, broadleaf, pate, large-leaved coprosmas, fungi), severely or to local extinction when at high numbers, and prevent their regeneration. **Social behaviour** Antlers grow under velvet September–December; velvet dries and is shed January–March; size of hardened antlers and number of tines indicate age and condition of males. During rut, antlers and body size used to judge opponents' strength; fights avoided by roaring and posturing contests, leaving little time for feeding throughout April (many males lose 20–30% of body weight during rut). Strongest, evenly matched males engage in vigorous antler-pushing, sometimes ending with a lethal swipe. Hinds and stags form separate groups except during rut; females stay in or near mother's home range for life, males disperse. At height of post-colonisation irruption, groups of hinds/young often 50–150 strong, stags 20–30; now most live in groups of 2–3. **Reproduction** Male groups disband March–April, adults move to rutting areas, compete for harems until May. Gestation 221–252 days, longer when food scarce. Females can breed at 2–3 years, males not until much older. In November, calves of previous season driven away by hind; new calf born December, remains hidden for first 5–10 days, mother-calf pair rejoins herd at 2–4 weeks; calf grows to 85–95% adult size by age 2 years, continuing slowly at least until age 7. All measures of fertility, growth rate and survival closely correlated with body size/condition, as determined by numbers and food supplies. Natural lifespan can reach 12–14 years for males, 15–20 for females. **Populations** Initial irruptions took red deer populations well above sustainable levels (to 15–30 deer/sq km) by 1950s–60s; the consequent natural crash was induced by starvation, reduced fertility and poor survival; after 1970s aerial hunting reduced numbers further (peak harvest 130,000 in 1974, dropping to 13–32,000/year in 1988–99), with great benefits for body size and productivity. Long-term, stable numbers in native forest *c.* 3–4/sq km (2–5/sq km in South Island, 5–15/sq km in North Island, depending on level of harvest). **Status** Introduced. **Management** Mixed. Major pest when at high numbers; along with possums and goats, deer help reduce density of woody stems in subcanopy, alter forest composition, expose forest floor, and accelerate erosion, but all these effects are less damaging now than in the past, because sustained hunting keeps numbers low and browsing effects more tolerable. Highly preferred species still survive in inaccessible places, and alpine grasslands are recovering. Deer carry bovine TB but probably could not maintain it if it were eradicated from possums. Greatly valued for commercial/recreational hunting; DoC issues >60,000 recreational hunting permits/year, and in 1988, 31,000 hunters took 42,000 red deer. Deer farms (legal in NZ only since 1969) specialise in producing venison on fertile arable land, and world-class sporting trophies on enclosed but natural mountain lands.

Wapiti *Cervus elaphus nelsoni*

Family Cervidae. **Identification** Antlers round, erect, 12+ tines; coat plain red-brown with dark head/neck in summer, grey-brown with dark mane on males in winter; rump patch large, extending onto lower back, creamy-white; tail short, creamy white; calves spotted for first 2 months. Wapiti are the largest round-antlered deer in the world, therefore a greatly valued game animal. Formerly believed to be a larger North American relative of red deer, but classed as a separate species; now recognised as only a subspecies representing one end of circumpolar cline in red deer body size, increasing from Scotland (the smallest) through Germany and Russia to Canada. Dental formula I0/3, C1/1, Pm3/3, M3/3 = 34. **Similar species** No other deer has a white-cream rump patch large enough to extend onto lower back. **Size** Adult males 200–260 kg depending on age, length 2 m; females 80 kg. **NZ range** Single group of 18 wapiti from Canada (Wyoming stock) released at head of George Sound, Fiordland, in 1905; spread to occupy 100 sq km by 1925, and much of central west Fiordland (200,000 ha) by 1950. After 1930s red deer invaded same area; consequent hybridisation was unstoppable, and now pure-bred wapiti can be maintained only on farms. **Habitat** Native forest from sea level to alpine scrub and tussock grasslands. Can browse branches to a greater height above ground than red deer. **Food**, **Social behaviour** and **Reproduction** Similar to those of red deer, proportionately adjusted for larger body size. **Populations** Since 1970, accelerating hybridisation with red deer has eliminated pure wapiti stock from the wild. **Status** Introduced. **Management** Mixed. Highly valued for recreational hunting, but also officially classed as a pest. To maintain the greater trophy value of wild wapiti for the benefit of recreational hunters, selective culling and selective commercial operations (1973–94) slowed the loss of wapiti-type animals. The deliberate management of wapiti for hunting in Fiordland National Park has created conflicts of interest between hunters and conservationists, still unresolved.

Bull.

DEER

DEER

Family Cervidae. **Identification** Antlers round, erect, eight tines; coat bright chestnut-red-brown, spotted in summer, plain brown in winter; black dorsal stripe; white rump patch, medium size, bordered with black, flared into prominent larger area when alarmed; tail long, white with black stripe; calves spotted. Prominent tufted metatarsal scent glands on lower rear legs. Dental formula I0/3, C1/1, Pm3/3, M3/3 = 34. **Similar species** Red deer has plain brown adult coat, black-bordered creamy rump patch, short brown tail; wapiti has plain brown adult coat, large creamy rump patch extending onto lower back, short white tail; sambar has plain brown adult coat, large rounded ears, small creamy-white rump patch, long

Stag.

brown tail; rusa has plain brown adult coat, small light brown rump patch, long brown tail; fallow has spotted or plain coat in several shades of brown to black, white or brown rump patch, long black and/or white tail; white-tailed deer has plain brown adult coat, white rump patch, long brown tail with white fringe. **Size** Males 60 kg, carcase 40 kg, length 1.4 m, height at shoulder 90 cm. Females 50 kg, 30 kg, 1.3 m, 80 cm. **NZ range** Founding group of six sika gifted to NZ by Duke of Bedford from Woburn Abbey herd (stock originally from Japan); released in 1905, with a calf born en route, in Kaimanawa Mountains east of Lake Taupo. Dispersed rapidly, now cover *c.* 6000 sq km, still extending with (illegal) help from hunters; new populations eradicated if found by DoC. **Habitat** Beech and mixed forest, grassy river flats, occasionally out onto open tops. **Food** Similar to other deer. In Japan, sika prefer open grasslands, but in NZ are constrained by hunting pressure to keep under cover of forests. **Social behaviour** Most live in single-sex groups or alone except during rut (March–May), when older stags are territorial. Antlers cast in November–December, new ones start growing at once, hardened by March. When alarmed, sika whistle shrilly and bound away with rump patch flared. **Reproduction** Calves born November–January; smaller in body size than red deer, so mature faster, and can more often achieve good condition on a given food supply. Often hybridise with red deer where their ranges overlap; where food is short, sika do better than, and may replace, red deer. **Populations** Smaller deer can achieve higher numbers, which makes them attractive to hunters, but also increases extent of browsing damage. Not suitable for farming. **Status** Introduced. **Management** Mixed. Valued for recreational hunting; also officially classed as a pest.

Sambar deer *Cervus unicolor*

Family Cervidae. **Identification** Antlers round, simple, erect, six tines; large body, plain dark brown in summer, darker brown in winter, males with a distinct mane; broad bare muzzle, large rounded ears; prominent pre-orbital and metatarsal scent glands; rump patch small, creamy-white; tail long, dark brown; calves plain. Dental formula I0/3, C1/1, Pm3/3, M3/3 = 34. **Similar species** No other large-bodied deer has large rounded ears and a long brown tail without rump patch. **Size** Adult males 230–240 kg, length 2–2.1 m, height at shoulder 1.1 m; females 115–160 kg; height 1.4 m; calves *c.* 5 kg at birth. **NZ range** Two separate populations established in 1875 and 1876, both from same Sri Lankan stock. Present herds occupy *c.* 600 sq km in coastal Manawatu /Rangitikei from Levin to near Wanganui, and *c.* 1500 sq km in Bay of Plenty from Rotorua to Whakatane. **Habitat** Farm shelterbelts, gullies, swamps and bush patches; native and pine forests. Can jump almost any obstacle with apparently little effort. Habitat damage minor and local. **Food** Grass, crops, browse bark, flax, almost any coarse herbage. **Social behaviour** Semi-social, nocturnal. Adult males solitary except in rut; then mark out a territory defended against other males. They do not collect a harem but attract females by roaring, consort with them briefly, then become solitary again. Females and younger males live in small family groups of 2–5. **Reproduction** Indefinite breeding season typical of tropical deer retained in NZ herds; mating and calving can be observed at almost any time of year; stags in velvet can be observed at same time as stags in hard antler, and some may keep antlers for more than one season. Hybridisation with red deer rare. **Populations** Limited mainly by hunting, also by agricultural development. **Status** Introduced. **Management** Mixed. Protected for recreational hunting under licence; Manawatu harvest *c.* 40–50/year, controlled by ballot system issuing on average 275 permits/year. Also a minor pest causing damage indistinguishable from that due to red deer living in same areas.

DoC

Stag.

Rusa deer *Cervus timorensis*

Family Cervidae. **Identification** Antlers round, erect, six tines; coat plain red-brown; rump patch small, light brown; ears pointed; upper lip pale; tail long, brown; calves plain. Dental formula I0/3, C1/1, Pm3/3, M3/3 = 34. **Similar species** Sambar is larger, has plain brown adult coat, large rounded ears, small creamy-white rump patch, long brown tail. **Size** Adult males up to 120 kg, 1.0 m at shoulder; females 70 kg, 0.8 m. **NZ range** Introduced from New Caledonia by accident, mistaken for sambar; original stock from Java via Mauritius. Eight individuals liberated near Galatea (Bay of Plenty) in 1907 established a herd that remained restricted to that area until after 1960, then it increased in numbers and expanded to present range of *c.* 570 sq km, including parts of western Urewera ranges. **Habitat** Scrub-hardwood forest, patches of bracken/manuka, now extending into tall podocarp forest. Prefers scrub for cover within easy reach of pasture for grazing. **Food** Grass, crops, some browsing. **Social behaviour** Semi-social, nocturnal. Females and young normally live in small family groups; males collect a harem during winter. In rut, males wallow and roar, and deliberately entangle bundles of vegetation in their antlers; confrontations between males that are not resolved by intimidation may

Stag (top); hind (above).

develop into a vicious fight. Stags cast antlers December–January; new growth complete and clean by May. **Reproduction** Rut July–August; gestation 249 days; calves born March–April. **Populations** National population *c.* 1000, annual harvest *c.* 200. **Status** Introduced. **Management** Minor value for hunting, minor pest.

Fallow deer *Dama dama*

Buck, black phase.

Family Cervidae. **Identification** Antlers palmate (70–80 cm long, 20 cm wide, with multiple tines) in adults, round in juveniles (20–40 cm); coat colour has four distinct phases (dark brown-black or white, both unspotted, and mid-brown or pale brown, both spotted in summer); rump patch medium size, white or brown, top half edged with black; small body, tail long, black or white; fawns spotted. Mature males much larger than females, with no mane, but larynx ('Adam's apple') and tufted pizzle (penis) sheath are prominent. Dental formula I0/3, C0/1, Pm3/3, M3/3 = 32. **Similar species** No other deer has varied colour phases, or palmate antlers and prominent larynx in males. **Size** Live (farmed) adult males 60–70 kg; wild males (carcases) 35 kg, body length 1.5 m, height at shoulder 1.0 m; female carcases 20 kg; 1.4 m; 0.9 m. **NZ range** The most widely distributed deer in NZ after red deer. Between 1860 and 1910, at least 24 successful releases (total 50–60 animals of European stock and their progeny) led to established wild herds. By 1980s, 10–13 separate herds remained, but escapes or releases from farms (legal over most of the mainland) have established many new wild populations. Where possible, and especially in areas such as Northland which are largely free of other deer, new groups are eradicated. Absent from most islands except Kaikoura and D'Urville. **Habitat** Forest, scrub, bush/pasture margins, pine plantations, rough or improved grassland, mainly at lower elevations, seldom above timber line. **Food** Wide variety of grasses, herbs and browse. Can cause severe habitat damage when at high density. **Social behaviour** Strongly sociable; at peak numbers in 1950s, some herds reached 100+ deer of all ages, both sexes; now groups of >3–4 are rare. When alarmed, females 'bark' loudly, adopt an 'alert' posture copied by others, and move off with an exaggerated bouncing gait. **Reproduction** Rutting males groan rather than roar, establish rutting territories in April–May, containing several muddy

110

scrapes surrounded by thrashed and scent-marked bushes. Antlers shed in October–November, new ones grown by February. Females not herded into harems, but choose from among displaying males. Gestation 234 days, most fawns born December, weaned at 4–9 months. Wild populations very productive where food supplies good; pregnancy rate in adult females can be 90%. **Populations** Well away from hunter access points, numbers can reach 18–20/sq km. In 1988, national breeding herd *c.* 8000–10,000. **Status** Introduced. **Management** Mixed. Shifting human attitudes have labelled fallow an asset (1860s–1930s), pest (1930s–80s), valued resource in designated Recreational Hunting Areas, e.g. Blue Mountains (1980s), and back to pest (since 1990s). Like wapiti, fallow are central to the ongoing conflict between hunters and conservationists. In Woodhill Forest (private land), an organised fallow hunting season runs over 3 months; *c.* 3000 hunters/year enter ballot for 640 positions, harvest 20–30 deer; trophy fallow shoots also offered by large enclosed game estates. Fallow farming began late 1970s with 10,000–15,000 wild-captured stock, improved since 1985 by imports of superior European and Mesopotamian strains.

Spotted buck with herd of mixed-coloured does and fawns.

Hinds, pale brown spotted phase.

White-tailed deer *Odocoileus virginianus*

Family Cervidae. **Identification** Antlers round, curving forward, 8+ tines; coat plain red-brown in summer, grey brown in winter; rump patch medium size, white; tail long, brown with white fringe, can be held upright as a conspicuous flag; prominent metatarsal glands; calves spotted. Dental formula I0/3, C0/1, Pm3/3, M3/3 = 32. **Similar species** No other deer has forward-curving antlers or uses white underside of tail as a flag. **Size** Adult males 55 kg, females 40 kg; length 1.5 m both; fawns 2 kg at birth. **NZ range** Original stock imported in 1905 from New Hampshire, USA; released in two groups of nine each, both established wild herds. The Wakatipu herd, starting from Rees Valley, inland Otago, has spread over 350 sq km of eastern Southern Alps; the other occupies much of eastern coastal forest of Stewart Island below 300 m elevation (over 1650 sq km). These deer are good swimmers so they live on or visit many smaller islands off Stewart Island. **Habitat** Wakatipu herd lives in low-elevation beech forest and adjacent river flats. On Stewart Island, where beech forest is absent, they live in mixed podocarp-hardwood forests. **Food** Mainly browsers, cannot survive on grass alone; prefer a diverse diet varying with season, including broadleaf, supplejack and coprosmas. **Social behaviour** Sociable. Females and offspring live in family groups, males separately. Extremely cautious; when alarmed, flee with white tail flag exposed. Males do not roar, but search for individual females and follow receptive ones, occasionally bleating. **Reproduction** Rut April–May. Gestation 187–222 days; calves born December; weaned at 2–3 months. **Populations** Wakatipu herd has declined from much too large (850 deer, *c.* 8/sq km, all in poor condition) in 1974, to 20–100 in 1980s; protected from hunting since then but has not recovered. Stewart Island

herd also irrupted and declined through 1970s, but numbers remain high in preferred areas (e.g. 18/sq km or more around Port Adventure and north-west coast). **Status** Introduced. **Management** Stewart Island herd valued for hunting but also a minor pest. Annual harvest from Stewart Island *c.* 1600, but bodies and antlers smaller than in US. Wakatipu herd neutral.

Doe.

Glossary

adaptation The features of an animal which adjust it to its environment. Adaptations may be genetic, produced by evolution and not alterable by the individual within its lifetime, or the temporary result of responses by individuals to environmental conditions during their lifetime, particularly while they are actively growing, or, in adults, during the breeding season. Natural selection favours the survival and breeding success of individuals whose adaptations best suit them to average contemporary conditions, at the expense of those with less suitable adaptations.

adult A fully developed, sexually mature animal.

aerial hunting The practice of shooting game or pest animals (usually deer, goats, chamois, or tahr) directly from a helicopter in flight.

Antarctic Convergence The region between 50° and 55°S, where cold, dense Antarctic sea water meets and slides beneath lighter, warmer subantarctic water.

antlers (cf. **horns**) Deciduous bony outgrowths from the skull of a male deer, produced each year before the rut and shed like a leaf at a special 'break-point' afterwards. Covered in soft skin (**velvet**) while growing, but naked bone when mature.

arboreal Living in trees.

blastocyst A very early embryo, still at the stage of a hollow ball of cells floating free in the uterus.

bovid A member of the family Bovidae (in New Zealand, cattle, sheep, goats, chamois and tahr).

browsing Feeding on woody plants and ferns (browse), cf. **grazing**, feeding on grass.

carnivore A member of the order Carnivora (in New Zealand, the cat, dog, stoat, weasel, ferret, sea lion, fur seal, or any of the five true seals); hence a **carnivorous diet**, one that includes much fresh meat.

catastrophic moult Process in which all the old coat is shed in large patches, including skin, rather than by shedding individual hairs without damage to the skin.

caudal To do with the tail.

cline A gradual and progressive change in some attribute of a species (e.g. body weight), measured over a substantial geographic distance.

cohort A group of animals all recruited into a population during the same breeding season or birth pulse.

colony (of bat roosts) A roost used by many different individual bats of one species, together or successively (cf. **community**).

commensal Species of animals closely dependent on humans, e.g. rodents making use of man-made buildings or other resources, but still wild; cf. **domesticated**.

community Multiple species living together by partitioning the habitat, as distinct from many individuals of one species sharing a den or roost.

delayed implantation A period ranging from a few hours to 9–10 months, during which development of the blastocyst is interrupted, and it remains floating free in the uterus.

demographic compensation Increased productivity and survival of a population in response to artificially high mortality imposed by management (shooting or trapping). Pest species are adept at using compensation to cancel out the effect of control operations, by the subsequent or even during the same year.

dental formula A conventional shorthand means of summarising the number and arrangement of the teeth. The numbers of each of the four types of teeth, in each half of the upper and lower jaws, are given in order: I (incisors), C (canines), Pm (premolars), and M (molars), plus the total number of teeth, e.g. I3/3 means there are three incisors on one side of the upper jaw, and one side of the lower jaw also has three incisors.

diurnal Active in daylight.

DoC Department of Conservation.

domestic Individual animals of a domesticated species living under direct human influence (cf. **feral**).

domesticated Species which have been tamed and bred under human control for many centuries, often now distinctly different in form and behaviour from their wild ancestors (cf. **domestic, feral**).

dorsal On the back of an animal.

embryonic diapause (Cf. **delayed implantation**).

endemic Found only in a given country or area (cf. **native**).

exotic (of species) Not native (in New Zealand, includes humans and all species introduced with human help, either deliberately or accidentally).

eyeshine The reflection from the eye of a mammal caught in a beam of light.

feral Individuals or populations of domesticated species living in the wild, free of human control. Not correct if applied to any species which has never been domesticated.

fertility The number of young actually produced and reared to a specified age.

gestation Pregnancy.

grazing Feeding on grass.

haul-out site/hauling ground Beach or rocks used by seals for hauling out, but not for breeding (cf. **rookery**).

head–body length The straight-line length from the tip of the nose to the base of the tail, measured on an animal lying on its back.

hibernation Prolonged seasonal torpor, usually in a specially insulated winter nest, e.g. hedgehog (cf. **torpor**).

home range The area traversed by an animal in the course of its daily activities, whether or not it is defended from intrusions by other animals (cf. **territory**).

horns Permanent bony outgrowths, covered with a keratin sheath, from the head of a male or female bovid (cf. **antlers**).

hybrid The offspring of parents of different species or subspecies.

indigenous Native to an area but not confined to it.

insectivore A member of the order Insectivora (in New Zealand, only the hedgehog); **an insectivorous diet**, one that includes a lot of insects.

introduced Brought to New Zealand with human help, deliberate or accidental.

irruption The explosive increase in numbers, with or without extension of range, characteristic of opportunistic species when first colonising new habitat or during particularly favourable seasons.

IUCN The World Conservation Union.

IWC International Whaling Commission.

keratin The strong and flexible non-bony substance from which claws, hooves and horn coverings are formed.

lagomorph A member of the order Lagomorpha (in New Zealand, a rabbit or a brown hare).

lifespan Maximum age to which an animal can live in ideal conditions (e.g. in captivity) (cf. **longevity**).

lineage A sequence of species related through time.

longevity The age to which animals might live in natural conditions.

MAF Ministry of Agriculture and Fisheries.

mammal An air-breathing, warm-blooded animal with a four-chambered heart, and mammary glands in the female.

marsupial A member of the order Marsupialia (in New Zealand, wallabies and the brushtail possum).

metabolic rate The rate at which the chemical processes of the body proceed.

molar Posterior chewing tooth, or cheek tooth.

mustelid A member of the family Mustelidae (in New Zealand, only the weasel, stoat and ferret).

native A species having colonised New Zealand without human help, at any time from Tertiary to contemporary times, and now maintaining a self-sustaining population here (cf. **endemic**).

nocturnal Active at night.

opportunist A species adapted to take swift, short-term advantage of temporary resources.

os baculum Penis bone, characteristic of some male mammals.

parturition The process of giving birth.

pellets Hard, dry faeces produced by herbivorous mammals (cf. **scats**). Shape is often characteristic, e.g. pellets of many adult deer are convex at one end and concave at the other, giving a 'dinge-and-nipple' effect; pellets of possums are convex at both ends.

pest A species whose effects on native fauna or flora require mitigation by human management.

placenta A structure that connects the foetus through the wall of the uterus to the mother's bloodstream, and ensures the transfer of oxygen and nutrients to, and removal of waste products from, the foetus.

placental mammals Those having a well-developed placenta, i.e. all living mammals except marsupials and monotremes.

population A more or less definable interbreeding group of animals of the same species.

post-partum Immediately after birth.

prehensile Capable of grasping.

productivity The number of offspring produced in a stated time per breeding female or per population.

protected All harvesting prohibited (cf. **resource**).

recruitment Addition of animals, i.e. young generation, to a population

resource Harvesting permitted under permit.

rookery Beach used by seals for pupping and mating (cf. **haul-out site**).

rostrum The snout of a whale or dolphin.

ruminant A mammal with a multi-chambered stomach specialised for storing, regurgitating, and later remasticating vegetation, or 'chewing the cud'.

scats Faeces, usually of a carnivore (cf. **pellets**).

scent mark A site at which chemical messages are received and deposited by animals of the same species, in the form of urine, faeces or the secretions of specialised scent glands. Also the action of depositing such marks.

sodium monofluoroacetate (1080 poison) A non-accumulating toxin that rapidly breaks down in soil and water, widely used against pest mammals in New Zealand.

species A taxonomic unit comprising one or more breeding populations of animals that are distinct from related species and do not interbreed with them, or if they do, cannot produce fertile hybrids (cf. **subspecies**).

subfossil Remains of an animal or plant preserved but not fully mineralised (this distinction is no longer accepted).

subspecies A taxonomic unit comprising one or more breeding populations of animals that are distinct from related subspecies and do not normally interbreed with them, but if they do, the hybrids are fertile (cf **species**).

suid A member of the family Suidae (pigs).

sympatric (of two species) Living in the same place, or having overlapping distributions, without interbreeding.

taxonomy The science of naming and describing animals.

TB Tuberculosis, a serious disease of warm-blooded animals caused by a group of closely related bacteria, the *Mycobacterium tuberculosis* complex. *Mycobacterium bovis* is responsible for TB in cattle and other mammals, and *M. tuberculosis* is the primary agent of TB in humans.

territory A defended home range.

tines The points of a deer's antlers. The total is the sum of tines on both sides.

torpor A physiological response to stress (cold temperatures or shortage of food) in which metabolic rate and pulse are slowed to a fraction of normal, body temperature drops almost to that outside, and breathing is intermittent. Can be daily (in bats) or seasonal (in hedgehogs) (cf. **hibernation**).

ungulate A member of either of the two orders Perissodactyla (odd-toed ungulates) and Artiodactyla (even-toed ungulates).

vagrant A species which visits the New Zealand region but breeds elsewhere.

velvet (cf. **antlers**).

ventral The underside of an animal.

weta A New Zealand endemic flightless insect of the order Orthoptera.

Further reading

For more details and extended explanations, consult the following publications.

Baker, A. 1999. *Whales and Dolphins of New Zealand and Australia*, 2nd edition. Victoria University Press, Wellington.

Gibbs, G. 2006. *Ghosts of Gondwana*. Craig Potton Publishing, Nelson.

King, C.M. (Ed) 2005. *The Handbook of New Zealand Mammals*, 2nd edition. Oxford University Press, Melbourne.

Reeves, R., Smith, B.D., Crespo, E.A., di Sciara, G.N. 2003. *Dolphins, Whales and Porpoises: 2002–2010 Conservation Action Plan for the World's Cetaceans*. IUCN, Gland, Switzerland and Cambridge, UK.

Watson, L. 1981. *Whales of the World*. Hutchinson, London.

Acknowledgements

Almost all the information given here is summarised from the authoritative books listed above, all easily available through any public library. Although the primary sources (technical papers and reports) supporting the material quoted are not listed here, they can be easily identified from the annotated texts and reference lists available in those publications.

The publishers and author of this book acknowledge with great gratitude the patient labours of the 29 contributors to the *Handbook of New Zealand Mammals*, who collected and verified most of the data quoted here: G. Asher, I. Atkinson, A. Byrom, K. Clapperton, G. Clark, P. Cowan, M. Fitzgerald, J. Flux, D. Forsyth, W. Fraser, C. Gillies, R. Harcourt, J. Innes, C. Jones, C. King, B. Lloyd, J. McIlroy, E. Murphy, G. Norbury, G. Nugent, C. O'Donnell, J. Parkes, B. Reddiex, W. Ruscoe, M. Sanders, K. Tustin, D. Towns, C. Veltman, B. Warburton. The cooperation of Oxford University Press (Melbourne) is gratefully acknowledged for permission to draw on copyright information.

The author would especially like to thank Alan Baker for his advice on cetaceans, and Ken Ayers for help with proof reading and the index.

Index

Other titles in New Holland's Photographic Guide series:

Ferns
Lawrie Metcalf
978 1 87724 694 4

Sea Fishes
Wade Doak
978 1 87724 695 1

Wildflowers
Geoff and Liz Brunsden
978 1 86966 047 5

Trees
Lawrie Metcalf
978 1 87724 657 9

Alpine Plants
Lawrie Metcalf
978 1 86966 128 1

Birds
Geoff Moon
978 1 87724 658 6

Mushrooms and Fungi
Geoff Ridley
Photographs by
Don Horne
978 1 86966 134 2

Seashells
Margaret S. Morley
Photographs by
Iain A. Anderson
978 1 86966 044 7

Insects
Brian Parkinson
Photographs by
Don Horne
978 1 86966 151 9

Reptiles & Amphibians
Tony Jewell
Photographs by
Rod Morris
978 1 86966 203 5